Foreword

Computing Under Protest is for the reluctant computer user who needs to be dragged kicking and screaming into the computer age. This means approximately four types of people, in no particular order, who suddenly need to get to grips with a computer on their desk:

- Secretaries, whose Bosses have decided to computerise (whatever that may mean) and expect the equipment to be used straight away, with no training.

- Bosses, who don't want to show less knowledge than their staff.

- Self employed people, who are too busy to learn anything properly, and are not inclined to study anything anyway at the end of a hard day.

- Home-based professionals, or *teleworkers*, who keep in touch with the office by phone and fax and who have very little access to help and support.

All have one thing in common — wondering where to start!

The problem with computer manuals is that you need to know what you're looking for to get the best out of them; that is, you can't use them properly because you don't know what you're looking for in the first place! Any manuals you do get will usually be concerned only with the technical details of the computer you have, and possibly a list of commands available with the operating system that comes with it. Even if you get a good one, the information relating to one subject will be spread over several pages rather than being easily available in one area.

Also, many programs are actually tools of the trade for certain professions (e.g. accounts); unless you know a bit about the circumstances in which such programs are meant to be used, you won't be able to use them properly at all; the learning curve arises from the job you have to do, and not the computer.

The information within these pages is intended both to give you the idea of what to look for in manuals, and to collect together related information on subjects you need to know to get started. It deals with the *why* behind using computers (and software), so it's easier to get to grips with the *how*, which is also discussed to a lesser extent.

This works, because all the different types of personal computer likely to end up on your desk behave in very much the same way, despite what the advertisements say. Having said that, this book is geared towards the IBM PC and the operating systems on it, simply because it's the most commonly available (it doesn't mean it's the best by a long way). Other machines are not forgotten, but mentioned for comparison.

The book assumes you have a computer already and starts off gently with an introduction to the Personal Computer and the capabilities of any programs you may have. It gets progressively more technical, but don't let that put you off – it's meant to be that way because books that are too elementary tend to get thrown away. It's also a fact that most people, however much they claim "computer illiteracy", always want more once they have a little knowledge. You should find enough in this book, at least to set you off in the right direction.

It's best to read straight through the book first of all, without trying to remember anything, and then go over what you need in more detail. *Don't* expect to be properly productive inside a week, but this will actually be dependent on the amount of practice you get (or how pushy your Boss is!).

Although jargon has been minimised, sometimes it can't be helped, and you will find a Glossary at the back of the book that contains many technical terms.

Thanks to Ian Allen and all at Letraset.

This book is for Sue, who needs it most of all!

Phil Croucher

COMPUTING
UNDER
PROTEST:

The how-to guide for those who don't want to!

Phil Croucher

SIGMA PRESS – Wilmslow, United Kingdom

First published in 1993 by

Sigma Press, 1 South Oak Lane, Wilmslow, Cheshire SK9 6AR, England.

British Library Cataloguing in Publication Data

A CIP catalogue record for this book is available from the British Library.

ISBN: 1-85058-289-0

Printed in Malta by
Interprint Ltd.

Distributed by

John Wiley & Sons Ltd., Baffins Lane, Chichester, West Sussex, England.

Acknowledgement of copyright names

Within this book, various proprietary trade names and names protected by copyright are mentioned for descriptive purposes. Full acknowledgment is hereby made of all such protection.

Contents

General Introduction

Why use a computer?

You can quite easily use a typewriter for your letters, or work out your accounts on the back of an envelope. If you did both only occasionally, you would probably save yourself a lot of time and money by ignoring computers altogether.

However, they are very good at doing repetitive things. Being machines, they don't get bored and are quite capable of doing the same thing over and over again without complaining. If, therefore, instead of 1, you've got 1000 letters to write, and they all need to be addressed to different people and look as if they've been freshly printed, it's time to think about getting a computer to do it for you.

Similarly, if you regularly make quotations, and the only things that vary from day to day are the prices, you can have the computer remember what your standard business letter looks like and insert the new amounts as required (always supposing that you've kept it regularly informed of the changes!).

And that's the trick; not so much to get your work done by a computer (a word processor is easier to use than a typewriter anyway), but to have as much of it done by the machine as possible, so you can do something much more interesting with your time.

What is a computer, anyway?

Even a coffee machine is a computer in its own small way; you push a button, it calculates what you want and, if you're lucky, you may even get what you asked for! However, for our purposes, we will assume a computer to be the traditional 3-piece unit looking something like this:

Of course, not all of them look like that. Some are self-contained in one unit and may look rather like the one shown on the opposite page:

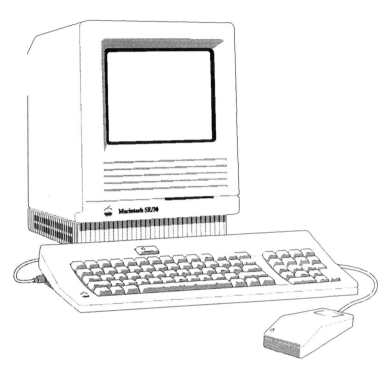

This is one of the Macintosh range, and you can see that the screen is built in to the cabinet. However, even Macintoshes come in three pieces, which consist of a *base unit*, where the working parts are held, a *screen*, which the machine uses to communicate with you, and a *keyboard*, which you use to communicate back.

The size of the base unit itself can vary, from a tall, floor standing unit (shown overleaf) to something slim that sits on your desk. The insides, however, will be more or less the same, as a computer is not necessarily more powerful just because it's got a larger case (some portables are very powerful indeed!).

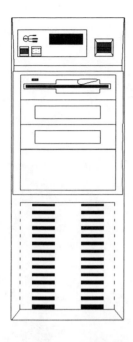

Note that you won't actually be using the computer to do your work, but the *software* that runs on it.

Software is the collective name for computer programs, or the electronic instructions that the computer obeys, and it's most important to realise from the start that the computer is just a machine controlled by software, which is ultimately controlled by you.

Hardware, of course, is the collective name for the machinery, and the two are bought separately; software doesn't come free!

Types of computer available

In the average business, there are two main types of computer you will come across, plus a couple of others.

IBM-compatible

This is the most common, but there are many brands that come under this umbrella. Whatever the name on the front, they are all supposed to conform to the standard set down by the original IBM Personal Computer (PC) in the 1980s, hence the term *compatible*.

You can relate this to video players if you like; machines may be made by different companies, but they all play the same cassettes, so you can take a tape from player to player and still watch the same film, provided the machines are compatible with the standards laid down by JVC.

So it is with IBM-type computers. Imitation IBMs are known as *clones*, and come from Taiwan and similar places, but there are several quality makes, notably Compaq, Dell, Zenith or AST, that are also available. They still have to run the same software to qualify as compatibles, but even this is no indication sometimes.

Many older machines used the MS-DOS operating system (see Chapter 3), as did (and do) those that follow the IBM standard. *Just because a machine runs this operating system, it doesn't mean that it's IBM compatible!* The essence of IBM compatibility lies in the way the machine is built; that is, the hardware must be made to a certain pattern, and things like printer connections should be where the software expects to find them.

Wherever you get them from, the rules about pricing apply to computers just as much as they do to any other commodity – you get what you pay for!

The more expensive types generally come through dealers (except Dell, and some others, who sell direct to the public) and you can expect the manufacturers to be around in the future because some of the profits go on improvements and support, so spares will be available later if you need them.

On the other hand, spares will be specially made and sometimes costly (this is especially true of portables and laptops). Although clone manufacturers come and go extremely quickly, their spares at least fit each other's machines easily, so even if your original supplier goes down the tubes, you can be reasonably sure of getting something else to fit.

Apple

The other type of computer you may come across is the Apple Macintosh. Nobody of any consequence clones these, and you will always get a genuine Apple if you go shopping for one.

They are usually sold through Apple dealerships, and can be expensive, but they are of good quality. Apple created their own niche market in the graphics and design fields, and there is a lot of very good software available. The Mac's distinguishing feature is the *Graphical User Interface* (or picture-based screen display) which hides the gory details of how it works from you (a pointing device that you run over your desk, called a mouse, controls a moving arrow on the screen to select pictures representing the programs you want to run – more in Chapter 3).

Others

Other machines can be used for business purposes, although they were built for other reasons, such as games, graphics or music. These would include (in no real order of suitability) the Commodore Amiga, Atari ST and the Acorn Archimedes.

Technologically, these are superb machines, and streets ahead of the Apple or IBM in many areas, even though some of the bits inside are actually the same (it's the way they're *programmed*, or told what to do, that makes the difference). However, they are specialised, and also have less software available that would be useful in a business. They can all pretend to be an IBM PC and run its software very successfully, but this is like buying a Bentley and using it like a Cortina — it's cheaper to buy the Cortina in the first place!

Regard these as being for professional computer users (like scientists) and enthusiasts only.

NOTES

The remainder of this chapter (actually the next two pages) is blank, and is meant for you to write odd notes in.

NOTES

NOTES

2

A Guided tour

The Keyboard

You've got to get information and instructions into the computer, and for this you use the keyboard. On IBM-compatibles, the 102-key version is now the most common:

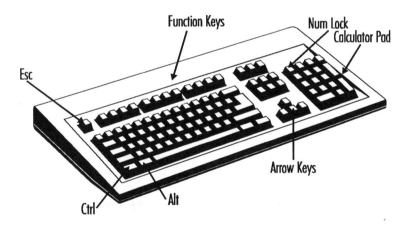

Most other computers follow the IBM line, and you will find their layouts generally similar, except on earlier designs.

The idea is that the words you type at the keyboard appear on the screen, but it's most important to realise from the outset that:

> **There is no one key which, when pressed, will cause everything to be wiped out!**

If you want to delete anything from the computer's storage space, you have to be very specific and issue the correct commands, which you will come across in Chapter 3. *You will not do any damage merely by touching the keyboard.*

There will be twelve *Function Keys*, which are used as short-cuts for instructions that are used most often. What those instructions are depends on what program you're running, but typically **F1** is used for Help, and **F10** saves your work so you can use it later.

NB ————

Over on the right hand side is a *calculator pad*, or *number pad*, which does two jobs; the < **Num Lock**> key on the top left of it determines which. You will notice that there are arrows and letters on some keys, as well as numerals; for example, number **6** has a right facing arrow, and **3** the letters < **Pg Dn**> (see left).

When the <**Num Lock**> key is pressed (and the little light somewhere on the keyboard comes on), the keys behave like a calculator pad, and you ignore the arrows and letters. When the light is off, however, the arrows and letters come into their own, and the pad issues *cursor control* commands (the cursor is a flashing block on the screen where the characters you type will appear — see Chapter 3 for more about the screen display).

On the 102-key keyboard, the number and cursor functions are split into two separate clusters, so you shouldn't need to bother with the <**NumLock**> key at all. You will see that the cursor control arrow keys are between the "QWERTY" keys and the calculator pad. Above the arrows are other short cut keys derived from the number pad, also in their own separate cluster. The two together look like this:

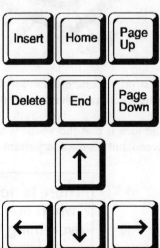

The short cut keys consist of:

< Insert >	This toggles *Insert Mode* on and off. When Insert mode is active, any text you type on the screen pushes text already there out of the way. When this is off, text already on the screen is overwritten.
< Delete >	This deletes any character that the cursor is positioned over.
< Home >	Takes you to the beginning of your work; especially applicable to spreadsheets.
< End >	Takes you to the end of your work.
< Pg Up >	Moves you through your work (towards the beginning) a page at a time. Sometimes this "page" will actually be a screenful, or about 20 lines.
< Pg Dn >	As above, but in the opposite direction.

The arrow keys simply move the cursor around the screen in the desired direction, that is, up, down, left or right, provided text is there already.

The QWERTY keys are so called because they have those letters on the left of the top row, and you treat them as if they were on a typewriter, except for two.

If you've ever used a typewriter, you will know that the **< Shift >** key does nothing by itself, but shifts the carriage so that you can print capital letters when you press any other key, where normally you would get lower case ones (the **< Shift >** key is on either side of the QWERTY keys on the row above the space bar, and usually has a thick upwards-pointing arrow, like the one on the left). Where a key has two symbols, the **< Shift >** key allows you to print the upper one.

For example, pressing a character key will normally get you the lower case version of what you want; push *p* and you get p on the screen. Hold down the **< Shift >** key and push *p*, however, and you will get capital P instead. Similarly, pushing the 6 key on the top row of the keyboard will get you 6, but use the **< Shift >** key as well, and you get the upper symbol on the key, which is ^ .

On a computer, there are two other keys that operate in a similar way, the *Control* and *Alternate* keys, called in books < Ctrl > and < Alt > respectively (at the bottom left of the keyboard).

The < Ctrl > key

The < Ctrl > key allows you to *control* part of what the computer does; for instance, holding down < Ctrl > and pressing S at the same time will sometimes save your work to disk (this actually depends on the program you use. Sometimes it moves the cursor one space to the left). In other words, using a < Ctrl >-*key* combination enables you to control some aspect of the operation of the computer, as opposed to just altering the screen contents. Sometimes, the ^ symbol is used to represent < Ctrl >, as in ^c for < Ctrl >-C. The Macintosh equivalent of the < Ctrl > key is the < Command > key, which has a funny symbol on it.

The < Alt > key

The other useful key is < Alt >, which produces *Alternate* characters instead of those already on your keyboard. For example, with some programs, if you hold down the < Alt > key and type *189* on the *number pad*, you will get the copyright symbol (©). The £ sign is < Alt >-156 (what characters you actually get will depend on your program — sometimes you need a 0 in front of the number as well).

Any characters not on your keyboard already can be obtained this way, because all letters of the alphabet and some symbols have each been allocated a number so that printers can be told what to print in a standard way.

In brief, the software sends numbers and the printer translates those into characters according to the country it thinks it's in.

The numbers are part of a code called ASCII (or the *American Standard Code for Information Interchange*). It's a bit of a mouthful, but the ASCII code is also useful as a bridge between different programs so you can exchange information between them.

Getting back to the keyboard, each key potentially has 4 levels of operation, when used either by itself, or with the < Shift >, < Ctrl > or < Alt > keys — it's a way of giving you 300-odd keys to play with even though there may be only 102 in front of you.

Other keys you need to know about are:

< Return >

This is the large key on the right hand side of the QWERTY keyboard (it's sometimes also called the **< Enter >** key).

It's used often, either at the end of every command, or for confirming selections you make with the arrow keys. In a wordprocessor, it works like the Carriage Return on a typewriter, putting you at the start of a new line to begin a new paragraph (but it doesn't send the screen shooting off several inches to the left!).

< Esc >

The **< Escape >** key is used almost as often as **< Return >**, but for the reverse. What it usually does is take you backwards out of a program the way you came in, without making any changes; however, it doesn't actually undo anything you may have started by pressing **< Return >**. It's at the top left of the keyboard.

< Backspace >

At the top right of the QWERTY keys, usually with a left facing arrow. It deletes characters to the left of the cursor, one at a time.

< Tab >

Halfway up the left hand side of the QWERTY keys, usually with two arrows facing in different directions.

Pressing this key moves characters across the screen to predetermined positions, usually 8 spaces at a time, but you can vary it. Useful for lining up characters in tables.

< Caps Lock >

Has the effect of keeping the **< Shift >** key down permanently, so you get CAPITALS when you type, but it doesn't affect the number keys (you must still use **< Shift >** to get the top character on these). Push the key again to release it. It's used for convenience when you need to type lots of capitals; for occasional capitals, just use the **< Shift >** key.

Maths functions

If you need them, maths functions are carried out with

+	addition
–	subtraction
*	multiplication
/	division

Note that there is no key called *any*, so if you see a message on the screen saying:

```
Press any key . . .
```

it means you can push any key on the keyboard — don't look for one with "any" written on it!

Stored keystrokes

As you progress, you will be using certain key sequences time and again, and you'll soon get fed up writing the same phrase or words several times over. To save your nerves, there is a way of combining keystrokes together so you can tell the computer (once only) that when you pressed a particular combination of keys, the sequence will be replayed at once (similar to getting a memory telephone to dial a number for you). This way, you can reproduce whole sentences or even sometimes a paragraph.

That is, you could store your name and address behind, say, the < Alt > -I key combination, and it would appear on the screen each time you pressed < Alt > and I together. Unfortunately, jargon crept in and stored phrases got called *macros* for some reason, but you could call them *Remember keys* instead. Each program has its own way of programming these keys, so you'll have to check their manuals for more information.

Stored keystrokes are called macros in wordprocessors and spreadsheets, but in databases they're called *procedures*. Operating systems such as DOS (see Chapter 3) use *batch processing* to do the same thing. Communications programs call them *scripts*.

Mice

As far as a computer is concerned, a mouse is a gadget that is run over a flat surface, such as a desk, which controls a pointer on the screen. You use the pointer to point at a picture of what you want the computer to do, rather than type broken English commands onto the screen from the keyboard. When you've found what you want, you press the button on the mouse (usually the left one, but the Macintosh only has one button, anyway) to make your selection.

Most programs can use a mouse in some way or another, and they do make life much easier in many ways. However, the keyboard still has its virtues, and neither is a complete replacement for the other. More about mice in Chapter 3.

The Screen

One way of getting information out of a computer is by displaying it on the screen. That's how you find out that it can't do what you want it to (and if you're lucky it may even tell you why!).

The quality of the image mainly depends on the screen's *resolution*, with a little help from how the computer is programmed to display it. Whether you can see sharp lettering or not depends on whether you have high resolution or not, and the better the standard of picture, the better your understanding with your bank manager needs to be.

Screen sizing is generally 80 characters by 25 lines, which is a hangover from the days when computers were programmed with punched cards — which all had 80 columns by 25 lines. By coincidence, this arrangement also suits the average size of TV screens, so the production line is easily diverted. If you're involved with graphic work, you will find A4 or even A3 sized screens, but these will be expensive, for technological reasons; as the same amount of screen information has to be spread over a larger area in the same amount of time, the screen must be run at a faster speed to cope. As with cars, speed costs money.

The Base Unit

This contains the thinking parts of the computer, as well as the *storage devices*, which are used to save your work for later (for more detail about the insides, see Chapter 9, *Under The Hood*). On the outside of the base unit, you will usually find a cluster of little lights and one or two buttons, of which one may be marked *Power*. If not, you can turn the computer on and off with a Big Red Switch, which may be at the front, or the rear, or on the right hand side.

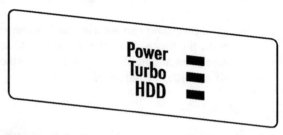

The buttons will typically be:

Power	Turns the computer On and Off.
Turbo	Computers now run very quickly, and this button slows the machine down to the "proper" IBM PC speed of 8 MHz, for programs that don't like to work too hard. Mostly, though, you can leave the turbo facility on.
Reset	If the computer freeezes up for any reason, the reset button is used to restart the computer from scratch without using the On/Off switch (to save wear and tear on the power supply). It's *not* used to reset the machine for somebody else after you've used it.

The lights are:

Power	Indicates whether the machine is on or off.
Turbo	Indicates whether turbo mode is on or not.
HDD	Indicates when the hard disk is being used. As the hard disk is permanently installed inside the machine, this is a useful aid to what's going on. It will flash often, but is nothing to worry about.

Chips

The brains of the machine will be a *microprocessor*, which will determine the family to which your computer belongs, because it will only understand instructions given to it in a particular language. There are also subordinate chips that each have a particular task to do, such as keep an eye on the keyboard, control the printer, etc. These jobs are handed down to them, rather like the way that tasks are delegated by a manager at work, although the main processor still controls how everything is done. In addition to the "worker" chips, there are also memory chips, which are used for *temporary* storage of information.

Memory

The memory contains the instructions that tell the main processor what to do. You could type the instructions in yourself, but this is extremely time consuming (assuming you get them right the first time) and you would never get your real work done, so programmers are paid to do the work for you. You then load (that is, copy) their program code into memory from the disk drives, and the instructions are fed to the microprocessor one at a time, extremely quickly.

The memory also contains the data created by your programs, so there is a constant battle for memory space between them.

Memory chips only remember things when the power is on, so any data stored in them when you switch the computer off will be lost, which is why disk drives are there; to make a more permanent copy of your work that you can use later.

Floppy Disk drives

Disk drives (where you save your work, or load program instructions from) operate like a cross between a video and a record player. They allow you to record and play back information on a plastic medium covered with a magnetic substance, similar to that on your video tape, but the disk is flat and round, so it also works like a record player – the recording head goes straight to a particular track, which gives you speed; you don't have to sit there for hours and hours while the tape winds through looking for what you want.

You insert and remove floppy disks to and from a disk drive, so they're the ones you pull in and out!

The first computers used 8" disks, which gradually got smaller with new technology, through 5.25" ones (on the left, below) into 3.5" ones (shown on the right). Although 3.5" disks are protected by a hard plastic case, they are *not* hard disks—more about those shortly. Disadvantages of floppy disks are that they are literally floppy, and thus easily damaged, with a large *access hole* in the outer casing that the record head needs to peek through to get to the disk surface—a prime candidate for fingermarks and coffee.

The 3.5" variety has this hole covered with a metal flap, but you still need to be careful. *Do not*, under any circumstances, take any floppy recording surface out of its protective cover, which is there for a purpose. If you require a "clean floppy disk", DO NOT take it out of its cover and run it under the tap!

Neither should you fold the larger type in half to get it into a hole meant for the smaller ones!

There is a notch on the side of 5.25" disks and a square hole on 3.5" ones—these are for *write protection* so you don't accidentally record over what's on there already (tape cassettes have the same system). The other hole on the 3.5" disk, if there is one, is to identify it as *High Density* or not, just like chrome tapes use a hole in the casing to operate a switch and identify themselves to a tape recorder.

There are two types of floppy disk, whatever size you have. Normal ones will be labelled as DD, meaning *Double Density*, and high capacity ones as HD, or *High Density*. The very first diskettes were *Single Density*, but technology moves on, and Double Density is now normal. HD disks are to DD disks what Chrome audio tape is to normal tape; they require a higher electrical current to record information, so it doesn't do to mix them up between disk drives, because the results will not be perfect.

A high density drive can use a low density disk, but the same is not true the other way round. Aside from asking an expert, the only way you can find out if you have a high capacity drive or not is to try and format a high density disk in it and see if it works, but most modern machines have high capacity drives as standard (High Density disks have the letters **HD** marked on them somewhere).

Before disks can be recorded on, they must be *formatted* (this is sometimes called *initialisation*). This is because there are so many types of computer that disks are supplied blank and it's left up to you to put them in the correct format.

When formatting, dummy information is placed on the disk in the right places, which is subsequently overwritten by any work you do, so when you format a disk you *completely erase what's there already*.

Different machines can get more information on the same size of disk; for example, the Macintosh is able to cram more information on to a 3.5" floppy because of the way the disk drives speed up and slow down as the recording head moves in and out from the centre. IBM drives rotate at a constant speed, and are less efficient.

Data is stored on disks in separate *files*. It doesn't matter whether it's program instructions or ordinary data, the space taken up by a particular set of computer code is still known as a file, regardless of the size, as long as it can be separately identified from other files (more about how to use files under *Everyday DOS* in Chapter 3).

Hard disk drives

Hard disks tend to be permanently installed inside the computer, and are called "hard" because the recording surface is made of metal (or glass), so they are considerably more robust than floppy disks, although they nevertheless require careful handling (treat them like eggs). The working parts are in a sealed metal case so no dust gets in.

They also work faster than floppy drives, and store upwards of 60 times as much data, generally speaking. It's like having a 20-hour cassette in your video player that you can't take out or replace.

Because of their special properties, hard disks need to be used differently; for example, because they're so big, data stored on them needs to be organised properly (into *directories*), otherwise you'll never find it again. Also, because they're permanent fixtures, data needs to be copied frequently off them to somewhere else, like floppy disks, for security reasons (this process is known as *backing up*).

Printers

Printers are an alternative method of getting information out of your computer (as opposed to the screen). Think of them as typewriters without keyboards; the instructions as to what to print come from the computer, although a keyboard is used to get them into the computer in the first place.

You won't have to program the printer, except when you write programs yourself (in which case you shouldn't need this book). The printer is controlled completely by your software, according to standard procedures. If you want *italic printing*, or **bold**, for instance, you tell your program, which sends the instructions on your behalf.

To do this, your programs need to be told what sort of printer they will be talking to, otherwise they will send the wrong commands, and the more common choices are mentioned below, although you should see if your software supports the badge on the front of it first (printers are also compatible with certain popular standards, in the same way that computers are).

You must also tell the printer itself what its identity is; this is usually done with mechanical devices called DIP switches (if you really want to know, the initials stand for *Dual In-line Package*).

Printers are connected to the computer in two ways. *Parallel printers* are by far the most common, and are sometimes called *Centronics printers*, after the company that invented the system of parallel data transmission, which uses eight wires at a time to transmit information.

Serial printers, on the other hand, only use one wire for data (but others to control the flow of it), so they can be slower, and more awkward to set up; however, they can be positioned further away from the computer.

Your software won't care which one you use; it's purely a personal matter between the computer and printer. For more about this, see Chapter 10, *Setting Up Your Own System*.

A printer must be loaded with paper before it will work — most of them make a Nasty Noise if they're empty. The printer must also be *on-line*, which is computer-speak for *Ready*, or in a state to accept instructions. Although most printers automatically go on-line after you switch on, you may actually have to push a button on the front.

Running costs are important. Although a printer might be cheap to buy, the cost of printing per page may well be extortionate in terms of consumables, such as ink or ribbons.

Paper

You might get *continuous feed*, or the *cut sheet* variety. Continuous feed is the stuff that comes with the holes down each side (see the picture of the dot matrix printer, overleaf), and cut sheet is what you put in a photocopier. Continuous feed is only used in dot matrix and some daisy wheel printers that have a *tractor feeder*. If a tractor feeder is installed, turn the platen friction *Off*, otherwise the paper will twist (in other words, let the tractor do the feeding by itself, and don't include the roller). It's possible you may come across a *cut sheet feeder*, which is used to supply the printer with cut sheets automatically, so you can go and have a coffee while it prints and not have to feed it by hand.

Continuous feed paper is best bought as *microperforated*, so it's easier to tear off the strips with the holes in.

Paper comes in various sizes, all of which have Meaningful Names (especially to laser printers). *A4* is a standard European size that is 11.69 inches by 8.27, and therefore has 70 lines if you use a density of 6 lines to an inch, which is fairly standard. On a laser printer, though, this may reduce to 60 because of the printable area available; finding out what you can actually print may take some experimentation.

Letter is an American size that is 11.5 inches by 8.5; similiar to, but not quite A4! The relevance of this lies in using laser printers with paper trays that only accept a certain kind of paper.

The printer is able to detect what sort of tray is fitted (and hence the size of paper), and if your software tries to print on a letter-sized page when you have an A4 tray fitted, you will get a continual prompting from the printer to load the right size of paper, but no printing!

The way to solve this is to enter the *Page Setup* routine of your program and change the page size.

Standard listing paper (used by programmers when listing their programs) is usually continuous feed. It has 66 lines per page.

The Daisywheel

Similar to a typewriter, where a preformed character on a wheel is impacted against a carbon ribbon, which then makes a mark on the paper. Output quality is high, but the machines are relatively slow and noisy. You can't print pictures, and they're out of date, but they are cheap as a result.

If in doubt, tell your software it's talking to a *Qume* (Sprint) or a *Diablo 630*. It could also work as a *draft printer*, but you may not get special effects (such as **bold** or *italic*).

Dot Matrix

A series of pins impacts against a ribbon and makes marks on paper, forming the characters. The earliest models used 9 pins to do this, but 24 pins and more are common, which gives better resolution (that word again) and sharper characters.

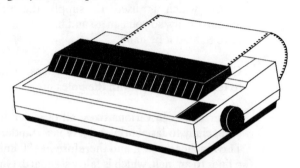

The output is just about acceptable for small business use, so dot matrix printers are more commonly used in a home situation. These printers can operate in several modes:

- *Draft*, where the characters are basic, but readable and printed quickly.

- *Near Letter Quality* (NLQ), which usually involves the print head passing twice over the area to be printed so you get darker, and better looking characters, but this both uses up ink and is slower.

- For pictures, the printer is switched into *graphics* mode, and driven directly by the computer. Sometimes, NLQ printing is done this way if you have typefaces that are not already stored in the printer's own memory banks.

If in doubt, set up a dot matrix printer either as an *Epson FX* or an *IBM Graphics Printer*.

Laser

Very high quality output, and fast. In use, a laser printer behaves just like a photocopier.

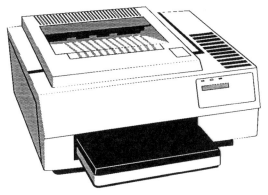

HP Laserjet is one standard setting, as is *Postscript*, but some laser printers can also emulate commonly available dot matrix printers, such as Epsons.

Inkjet or Bubblejet

A fine spray of ink is used to form characters. Very good quality, nearly as good as laser printers, but around half the speed. Sometimes the ink is washable, and large black areas can make the paper soggy. Good value, and colour versions are available.

At a pinch, you can use fountain pen ink in the cartridges (use a syringe to get it in there), but the ink will take longer to dry because of the lack of alcohol.

Thermal

Hot needles impacting on a wax ribbon. Mostly used for colour printing, and expensive to run. Thermal printers also need special paper.

Modems

These connect computers to the telephone system so they can communicate over long distances – instead of talking, you just type your messages on the keyboard. The main reason for doing this is for sending data; very often it's cheaper than using the mail. For example, instead of printing and posting their work (often difficult in a war zone!), journalists regularly send their copy direct to Head Office over the telephone, which at least saves them carrying a printer as well. Modems are needed because computers speak digital language, whereas telephones don't; a conversion is therefore needed between the two.

      The modem may be outside the computer, or plugged inside the casing. Some modems have fax capabilities as well, so you can send faxes directly without printing them first. You don't just save paper; fax/modems can usually be programmed to transmit faxes at predetermined times to any amount of numbers automatically, which is great for sending lots of messages overnight when the rates are cheap.

      More about communications in Chapter 8.

Tape Streamers

These are nothing more or less than tape recorders that take a recording of the contents of your hard disk for backup purposes, so the tape cartridge does a similar job to a video cassette. In theory, if your hard disk becomes inoperative, you can restore the contents with the least inconvenience by just replaying the tape to the new one.

      A tape cartridge looks like this:

Networks

A network is a number of computers joined together by cable so that they can talk to each other. It's the same as having a phone system, except that the network is usually internal to the building. The idea is that, since they can transfer data between themselves, they can also share other things, like printers, that would otherwise be idle if only used by one machine. Typically, one machine will have the printer attached to it, and all the others will send their print jobs over the cable.

Computers joined together by cable are called *workstations*.

Multi-user concepts

When several people (and computers) have to work together, a few procedures must be followed, otherwise things get disorganised. You must inform the system of your presence by *logging in* with a valid *user name* and *password* before you can use it. This is both for security purposes and to ensure that resources are allocated fairly between yourself and other people. Your user name and password will be issued to you by a *Supervisor*, who is somebody appointed to look after the system.

Privileges

Once you've logged in, what you are allowed to do and where you are allowed to go is determined by the Supervisor; you will have your own storage area to work in with automatic *privileges* granted to you. For example, you will typically be able to modify your own work in your own area, but you won't be able to do anything to anyone else's unless you are given permission.

Logging Off

When you want to stop using a network, you must *log off*, because the equipment can only handle so many people, and you may need to make way for others.

3

Operating Systems and Software

A computer is only a machine, so it needs instructions to run itself; for example, it can only put letters on the screen after you press a key if it's told to. However, it's a waste of time writing the same sort of instructions for every program, which is why computers have operating systems. These are really *collections* of programs that perform various standard housekeeping tasks, such as translating keypushes into screen displays, changing the colours on the screen, or simply copying data from one part of the computer to another. Other software is then written up to the operating system level, without worrying about what sort of hardware it's dealing with. This saves programmers producing the same code that everyone uses over and over again.

Although an operating system is technically a program, in that it contains instructions that tell the computer what to do, it's not one in the sense that's commonly understood, as one that actually does work for you. The distinction is therefore made between *the system* and *application programs*, or programs that can be applied to a task. Applications concern themselves with *what* is to be done, whilst the operating system worries about *how* it's to be done.

Unfortunately, it's pretty boring just sitting and looking at the system screen—*you must load an application program on top of the operating system before you can do anything useful with your computer*. The sequence is therefore to load DOS first, then whatever program you want to run.   See next page

However, you still need to know at least the basics of how the operating system works, if only because your applications use it and you need to know what they're getting up to (this includes *Windows*). You especially need to know about *directory organisation* and *file management*, because you will want to keep track of where your work is.

DOS

On an IBM-compatible, the Disk Operating System (or DOS), is the program that's running when nothing else is; it's the one that starts the computer before you can load another. If you like, it's the set of instructions that tell the machine it's a computer and not a coffee machine! It's called the Disk Operating System (or *System* for short) because, in the early days, the disks needed the most management, but gradually the remainder of the computer got thrown in as well.

Every computer has an operating system, and they ultimately all do the same job. Some are more user-friendly, though (on the Macintosh), and some are downright user-hostile (like Unix). That used on IBM-compatibles is commonly called DOS, and mostly lies somewhere in between.

User-friendliness is not necessarily a boon, however. Ease-of-use and automation take up processing power that could sometimes be better used elsewhere. Although not as easy to learn, DOS is fast, especially when the commands you use become reflex actions.

Note that you have to buy DOS, just like any other software. It doesn't automatically come with the computer!

There are two versions of DOS. Both do the same job and use the same commands; they're just made by competing companies and each has one or two more services than the other. Only the common denominators will be mentioned in these pages, however, and everyday DOS commands are discussed later in this chapter.

MS-DOS

This version of DOS is written by *Microsoft*, hence *MS*. Microsoft wrote the first DOS on behalf of IBM for the IBM PC but, after version 4, Microsoft began to market DOS themselves.

DR-DOS

The *DR* stands for *Digital Research*, whose product can be regarded as being Microsoft-compatible, as it came later. They have a small, but important, corner of the market.

Graphical User Interfaces

In an effort to help the learning process, *Graphical User Interfaces* have been designed to make computers both easier to use and more standardised in the way they work.

good

Like DOS, a GUI is not a computer program in the traditional sense of the word; for example, you can't use it directly for wordprocessing or anything else you might want to use a computer for. Rather, it's a program that provides a *working environment* for "real" programs to operate in, as DOS does. In fact, GUIs can be regarded quite simply as operating systems with pictures.

The general idea is to use symbols (called *icons*) to represent the programs available. A pointing device, like a mouse, is used to control an arrow on the screen which indicates the program you want to run. It's then executed by "clicking" the mouse button or pressing the < Enter > key.

N B

Of course, the Macintosh has been using a graphical interface ever since it was created, and the pictures are actually part of the operating system, so performance is optimised. GUIs used on IBM-compatibles, on the other hand, sit on top of DOS and actually use some of its facilities, so you still need to know some DOS to get the most benefit from a GUI.

Windows

Windows, written by Microsoft, is based on the idea that as you go through your working day your desk gets progressively cluttered up with pieces of paper which pile up on top of each other. As your attention gets drawn to one or another piece of paper, you will pull it out and place it on top.

With Windows, a program will occupy its own little *window* on the screen, which can be moved, or made bigger or smaller to suit your requirements (hence the name of the program).

If you need to use another program, you don't need to close down the first; just open another window, which can be on top of the previous one, or clear of it so you can see them both at once on the screen. When you've finished, just bring the first back to the front again, as you would with your piece of paper.

Another benefit of using a Windows-type system is the uniformity — the menu will generally be the same from program to program, so even if you start using new software, you can do basic things (such as load documents, etc) quite easily.

You can have as many windows as you like, subject to:

- The size of the screen, and

- The ability of your computer to support them

A typical Windows screen looks something like this:

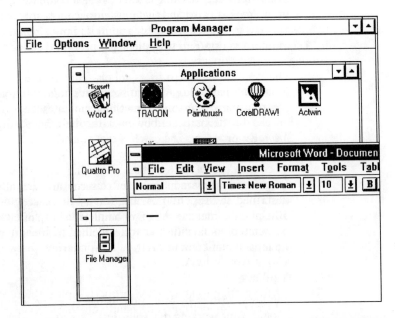

The box (or window) marked *Applications* is a *group window* containing *icons* representing programs available. The one marked *Microsoft Word* contains a running program (a wordprocessor).

Each window can be moved anywhere on screen, made larger or smaller, to occupy the whole screen (*maximised*) or collapsed completely (*minimised*). A minimised program is merely in suspended animation and can be recalled at any time; you will be at the place you left off. Running several programs at once means you don't need to close down one program before opening another, which greatly improves productivity. *Windows* also gives you the ability to *cut-and-paste* between programs; that is, you can *cut* data from one place and *paste* it to another.

There's no point in discussing how to use *Windows* further, as there's an excellent tutorial supplied with the system, available via the *Help...* menu.

Everyday DOS

Although much of what DOS does is automatic, you can override it with various commands which are supplied for that purpose. As with application programs, approximately 10% of DOS is used for 80% of the time, so of the 160 or so commands that you could get involved with, you only really need to bother with about 18 for day-to-day use, which is what the rest of this chapter is all about. Of that 18, around 10 are generally used only when the machine is started up, and you can get it to run those on your behalf anyway. You will also find that most application programs can get DOS to do what you want, and in a much friendlier and more powerful manner, so the task of operating a computer (as opposed to just using a program) suddenly becomes not quite so daunting as it first appears.

> You don't have to read the rest of this chapter all that thoroughly if you're using *Windows* or something similar, because it will carry out all the functions described in it through the services of the *File Manager* program. The catch is that you still need to know what you *can* do, so you can get *Windows* to do it!

> DOS commands mentioned in this chapter are more completely described in Appendix A, but for a full description, refer to the official DOS manual. A fairly complete list of those which can safely be deleted to save disk space, together with short descriptions of what each one does, in case you're wondering what you're missing, is also in Appendix A.

> As for getting to know DOS properly—please note that there is no substitute for getting your hands on the keyboard and *using* the information given in these pages!

Starting a computer with DOS

The computer is started with a *System Disk*, which is one that contains DOS. This process is known as *booting*, so the disk which kicks the machine into life is also called the *boot disk*. Because it contains the operating system, which naturally takes up room, you won't be able to get as much data on to a system disk as you would on to an otherwise empty one.

Disk drives available

The boot disk can be either a floppy or a hard disk. On an IBM-compatible, disk drives are labelled A, B and C, with any additions using subsequent letters in alphabetical order.

Although you can have drive letters up to Z, anything above E will more than likely belong to those on other computers which you can get to from yours, such as those on a network.

Drive letters have a colon after them (e.g. A:, B:, C:, etc). This is to make sure that the computer knows you're talking about a *device* (a disk drive in this instance) and not just a letter of the alphabet.

Any time you issue an instruction containing a drive letter to the computer, you must include the colon, to avoid confusing it (you will find the colon on the right hand side of the QWERTY keys, above the semi-colon, so you'll have to use the < **Shift** > key as well).

Drive A: is always the first floppy drive, and B: the second (if you have one). The first hard disk is called C:, the second D:, and so on. If you have no drives at all on your computer, you're probably on a *network*, and may be using drives belonging to other computers that are connected to yours, in which case the System is loaded over the cable joining them. All you need to do is switch on.

You will generally see two types of IBM-compatible computer:

- One with up to two floppy drives only (A: and B:).

- One with a hard disk, and up to two floppy drives (e.g. A:, B: and C:).

Computers with up to two floppy drives

Switch the computer on and place the *System Disk* in drive A: (which is usually the one on the left, or the top). If you're not sure, it may have an *access light* on, waiting for a disk to be put in it. Be careful to keep the disk the right way round (label uppermost), and close the gate afterwards, to keep it in the drive.

The gate lever is on the front of the drive:

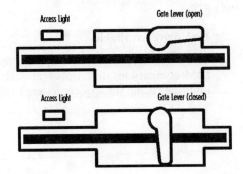

3.5" drives don't have a gate lever; they snatch the disk out of your hands and clamp it in automatically! However, they do have an eject button which you push to get the disk out (if you've got a Macintosh, all this is done electronically).

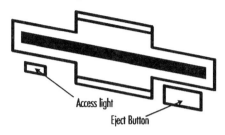

Access light
Eject Button

It's not a good idea to place the disk in the drive first and then turn the computer on, because closing the gate clamps the read/write heads to the disk; a small burst of electricity may get through and damage any data on the disk.

Computers with a hard disk (and floppy drives)

Just switch the computer on! Most computers are trained to look in the first floppy drive (A:) for an operating system, then to look elsewhere, traditionally to the first hard drive in the chain (C: on an IBM-compatible). If it can't find one at all, it will display a message on screen, asking for a system disk.

Date and Time

During the startup sequence, you may be asked to tell the computer the time and date (so it can keep track of when you create your work). This is because it has no other startup instructions (see Chapter 10). For now, though, press **< Return >** each time to get to the *screen prompt* (see below).

The Screen Display

Once the computer has started, you should see a screen display like the one shown overleaf.

If you don't get anything, it's possible your disk hasn't got a system on it at all, so you will have to refer to *How do I......?* (later this chapter) to see how to put one on, and come back here when it has.

If your machine launches straight into a program as it starts, you should get the same screen if you quit the program.

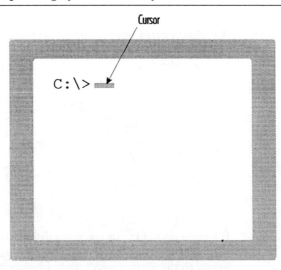

The screen contains the *system prompt*, so called because DOS (the system) is prompting you to do something, like give it a command. Just to make sure it gets your attention, there will be a flashing block next to it, called a *cursor*.

The line which the prompt and the cursor occupy is called the *command line*. This is where you type the commands you want the computer to carry out, including the names of any programs you may wish to load. Giving commands to DOS is the way you manually override many of its automatic functions.

Let's try one! Just to prove you're the Boss, we will change the prompt you see on screen. The command to do this is (oddly enough) called PROMPT.

Type this word now (it doesn't have to be in capitals), followed by your first name:

```
PROMPT FRED
```

(replace FRED with whatever your name is). After the command, press **< Return >**.

From now on, it will be assumed that you know to press the **< Return >** key after every command (it soon becomes automatic anyway). Notice that no superfluous words are used—DOS commands closely resemble broken English.

Your screen display should now read:

```
FRED
```

instead of:

```
C> (or A>)
```

Just for fun, type:

```
PROMPT ^B
```

If you remember, the ^B means hold down the **< Ctrl >** key and press B.

To get the prompt reading what it was before, just type:

```
PROMPT $p$g
```

The $ sign means that the PROMPT command is to supply special information. For example, if you were to use **$d**, PROMPT would get the date from the computer's clock for you. **pg** tells it to supply information about the *current drive and directory* and place the > sign at the end.

By now, you will have a lot of text on screen, so to tidy things up a little bit, type:

```
CLS
```

(plus **< Return >** !) which is short for **CL**ear **S**creen. Most computer commands are shorthand versions of the real words you would otherwise use, so quite often you can work out the name of the command you want to use by deducing it from what you want to do. For example, try the DIR command, which is short for **DIR**ectory, or a list of what is contained on your disk.

Type:

```
DIR
```

(don't forget **< Return >** !).

You'll probably see a long list of names flash past without you getting a chance to read them, but when it stops you might see something like:

```
Volume in drive C is GNOMAD
Directory of  C:\

COMMAND  COM     50456  9-11-91  8:09a
AUTOEXEC BAT       171 24-01-92  7:06p
LCD      IDX       473 25-01-92  4:52p
FORMAT   EXE      3432 30-01-92  7:44p
CONFIG   SYS       291 25-01-92  6:04p

     24 File(s)     5097472 bytes free
System files exist
```

This is a list of the data files contained on the drive displayed at the prompt. The *volume* is the electronic name given to the disk (for more about Gnomads, see the wordprocessing exercise in Chapter 4). Because you didn't include the drive name in the DIR command, the computer assumes that you mean the one displayed, in this case drive C:.

Very often, the list of files is so long that you don't get a chance to see it at all. You can vary the DIR command to help you read it properly, by adding a *command switch* to it.

A command switch consists of a forward slash (/) followed by a letter, such as P. For example, the command:

DIR /P

will cause the screen display to pause after every pageful (P means *Page*).

To get a *wide* display, type:

DIR /W

This will spread the information you want across the screen. Can you combine /P and /W? Try it and see!

Note that the Wide display doesn't carry as much information about what's on the disk as does the normal one.

Not every switch works with every command in the same way, but the common ones that do are:

page ?

/P	Display a screenful of data at a time.
/W	Produce a wide display.
/S	Exercise the command on associated sub-directories as well, but see the FORMAT command, which uses it to place the system on a disk.
/V	Verify that the command (usually COPY) worked properly. However, this will only check the *readability* of the data transferred, not whether what arrived was the same as what was sent (see COMP for that). You can issue a command called VERIFY to save yourself issuing this switch every time.
/?	Provide help (with later DOS versions only).
/h	As above.

Looking at other drives

If you wanted to see what was on a disk in another drive, for example B: (assuming there was a disk in it), you would have to include the drive letter in the command as well, like:

```
DIR B:
```

Notice the space between the two parts of the command. Commands are often split into several parts, usually what you want to do, and where, as shown above. The space lets DOS know how the command is split up, and is quite important, as you will find when you use more complex commands later.

If you actually want to run the above command now, make sure that you have a *formatted* disk in drive B: (see *Disk Formatting*, on p 39, if you're not sure about this).

Using other drives

You can check what the *current drive* is by looking at the command prompt, which may look like:

```
C:\>
```

This means that you are currently logged on to drive C:, in the *root directory* (directories are explained shortly).

Changing to another drive simply means typing its letter, followed by a colon and **< Return >**, e.g.

```
A:
```

This will change the current drive to A: and, if there is a disk in it, you will see the following prompt on your screen:

```
A:\>
```

Disk Access Lights

When a program is using a disk drive, the *access light* (on the front of the drive itself) will be on. Do not remove a floppy disk at this point, because there may be data in use that cannot be worked with again if it's damaged.

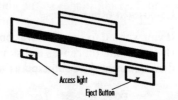

Access light

Eject Button

Always ensure that the drive access light is off and that no program has data in use before changing floppy disks.

Loading programs

Although the prompt displays the current drive (and directory), you can use programs on others merely by prefixing your command with the appropriate drive letter. For example, if you wanted to use the EDITOR program from drive A:, type:

```
A:EDITOR
```

from which it will load.

If you see either of these two messages:

```
Command or filename not recognised
Bad Command or Filename
```

the system cannot carry out your request because it can't find the program belonging to the name you typed. This could be because the program is not on the disk in the first place or, if it is, either DOS hasn't been told properly where to find it, or you have mistyped the name (you *must* be exact).

Some commands need extra information on the command line; for example, DISKCOPY requires to know FROM what drive and TO what drive when it is invoked:

```
DISKCOPY A: B:
```

really means:

```
DISKCOPY [from] A: [to] B:
```

Disk formatting

Unfortunately, you can't put data on a disk without preparing it first. Disks as supplied out of the box have to be made ready with a process called *formatting*, which lays down dummy information in the right places so the computer knows where to put the real stuff later. You can reformat old disks at any time, but any data on them will be *overwritten and lost!*

Place a new disk in the empty floppy drive, close the gate and type:

```
FORMAT B: (or A: if you have a hard disk)
```

DON'T type FORMAT just by itself without a drive letter! DOS may assume you mean the *current* drive and proceed to overwrite the contents of the disk already in there!

Remember the command says what to do (FORMAT) and where to do it (B: or A:), so don't forget the space between the two parts. Remember also **< Return >** !

You will be asked to place a new disk in the drive concerned; press **< Return >** if you're sure you've got the right disk in there and press **< Return >** to the question regarding *volume labels*.

When everything has finished, answer *N* to the question:

```
Format another disk (Y/N)?
```

Now type:

```
DIR B: (or A:)
```

again, to confirm that the disk is readable. You might see:

```
Volume in drive has no label
Directory of B:\

File not found.
```

Filenames

The word *file* (mentioned above in the directory list) refers to a separately identifiable set of computer code apart from any others, regardless of whether it is a real program, like a wordprocessor, or text, such as a letter to a bank. When you work with your programs later on, you will be creating your own files, so it's important to know how to work with them as soon as possible.

Have a look at one example from the directory list given above.

```
FORMAT.EXE
```

A file has a first and second name, so the complete *filename* is in two parts, separated by a full stop, although the full stop isn't displayed on the screen when the DIR command is run (it's replaced by a space).

The first part of a filename is up to eight letters long, and is the actual name of the file; the second has three letters, and tells the computer what type of file it is.

Normally, you shouldn't need to bother with this *extension*, as it's called, except when referring to the complete file as part of a command. Thus, a filename has the following structure:

```
filename.ext
```

Neither part of a filename should contain spaces, punctuation marks, or any of the following symbols:

```
~ = , : ; * ? @ " ' ' ^&
! % \ / $ [ ] ( ) . + |
```

Sometimes the computer uses these symbols or characters for its own purposes, and if you use them, you'll just confuse it. The easiest way to get out of remembering them all is simply to create filenames with numbers and letters only, with *no* spaces. Some file extensions, including the following, are reserved:

.$$$	A temporary or incorrectly closed file.
.TMP	When memory runs out, many programs write the extra bits to a disk, marking the files created with extensions like these, so it can remember what they were.
	Normally, you won't see these files, since they're deleted automatically when they're finished with, but if the computer is switched off while the program that created them is still running, they won't be erased properly, and will thus be visible when a DIR command is issued.
.BAK	A Backup file. When a program opens a file that already exists, a copy of the original is loaded into memory to be worked on, while the original file is renamed with this extension as a safety measure.
.BAS	A BASIC program.
.BAT	A batch file, containing commands executed in sequence.
.CMD	CP/M-86 program file (short for CoMmanD). Very ancient!
.COM	DOS program file (short for COMmand).
.CPI	Code Page Information file.
.EXE	DOS program file (short for EXEcuteable).
.SYS	Device drivers, used to tell DOS how to work with special equipment.

Some application programs may have their own reserved extensions, such as .GEM, .WK1 or .DBF. You will have to refer to their manuals for further information.

There are also combinations of letters that refer to *devices* used by computers, such as:

```
CON, PRN, AUX, NUL, COM, LST or LPT
```

To avoid confusion, the above should also not be used in filenames. If you're bothered, they stand for:

CON	CONsole (screen).
PRN	PRiNter.
AUX	AUXiliary.
NUL	A dummy device that fools the computer into thinking it's actually talking to something; it's the computer equivalent of a black hole to which you can send the results of a command when you're not bothered about them.
COM	COMmunications port.
LST	LiST device (usually a printer).
LPT	Line PrinTer.

File information

When you display the contents of a disk with DIR, there's a lot of information given about each file. Let's have another look at the list given earlier:

```
Volume in drive C is GNOMAD
Directory of C:\

COMMAND   COM    50456  9-11-91  8:09a
AUTOEXEC  BAT      171 24-01-92  7:06p
LCD       IDX      473 25-01-92  4:52p
FORMAT    EXE     3432 30-01-92  7:44p
CONFIG    SYS      291 25-01-92  6:04p

        24 File(s)    5097472 bytes free
System files exist
```

After the filename, the figures to the right indicate the size of the file, or how much space it occupies on the disk, in *bytes* (a byte is eight bits of computer language, and it takes one byte to place a single character on the screen). In the case of FORMAT.EXE, the file is 3432 bytes in size, or 3K for short. K is an abbreviation of *Kilo*, which is Greek for 1000.

After the size of the file are columns containing the date and time the file was created, which is useful if you've written two letters and have forgotten which one you worked on last.

At the bottom is how much disk space is free for more files.

Directories

Some drives have bigger capacities than others, and if you just deposited your files on to them in one great lump, you would never find anything again (also, if you typed DIR, the list would be so long you would never catch up with it all). Fortunately, you can split large drives up into smaller areas in which to place different files, so you can keep your wordprocessor data away from your DOS files, or otherwise organise your programs.

A portion of a disk is called a *directory*, and is referred to with a backslash (\), in the same way that the disk drive is referred to with a colon (:). Everything starts with the *Root directory* and works downwards.

Although the directory system works on any disk, it is mostly relevant to hard disks. In concept, it all looks like the diagram on the left. It actually looks like the diagram on the right:

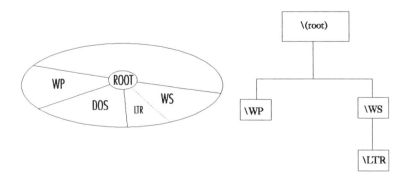

\LTR is a *subdirectory* of \WS. Multiple subdirectories are created below first-level directories, and the route from top to bottom is known as the *Path*.

A directory display in the *File Manager* program that comes with *Windows* would look something like this:

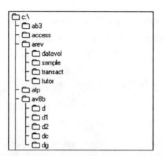

Directories have names as well, which are also eight letters long, but without the full stop and extension that filenames have. In a DIR display, they would appear with < DIR > next to them:

```
Volume in drive C is GNOMAD
Directory of  C:\

AB3           <DIR>      12-01-92   5:30p
AREV          <DIR>       7-02-92   5:02p
ARTLINE       <DIR>      12-01-92   5:30p
DOS           <DIR>      12-01-92   5:30p
AUTOEXEC BAT        381  16-03-92   4:54p
CONFIG   SYS        281  20-03-92   6:04p
DRMDOS   CFG       6030  19-02-92   2:58p

    30 File(s)     8525824 bytes free
```

The combination of a drive letter and directory name is known as a *Path description*, and usually includes the filename at the end.

As an example, a typical path on drive C: for the WS program, based on the diagram on p 43, could be:

```
C:\WS\WS.EXE
```

Here, the program file is in the \WS directory on drive C: (it helps if you give directories names that refer to what's in them).

Although you can have subdirectories off subdirectories, it's not advisable to go too deep, because eventually it becomes just as inconvenient to type the full pathname of any file as it would be to find it in the first place if everything was placed into the root directory (the prompt would also get so long it would take up most of the screen). In addition, your hard disk would have to work harder.

Keep the root directory as clean as possible, and use the PATH command (see later) to help the system find things.

Directory Management

There are three commands associated with directory structures, **MD**, **CD** and **RD**, and they are used to **M**ake, **C**hange to or **R**emove Directories respectively.

To create a directory *underneath your present level*, use:

```
MD directoryname
```

To change directories, just type:

```
CD\directoryname
```

Where *directoryname* is the name of the one you want to go to, which then becomes the *current directory*, or the one the computer is looking at directly.

You can jump up one level of subdirectories by simply typing CD .. (the two full stops are shorthand for the *parent directory*, or the next one up in the hierarchy), or by using the full pathname.

For example, referring to the diagrams on page 41, you can go from \WS\LTR to \WS by typing either of:

```
CD ..
CD\WS
```

In the above example, the \ means "go via the root", so to move sideways amongst *first level directories*, include the backslash (\):

```
CD\WP
```

You can get to the root from anywhere by using:

```
CD\
```

Removing directories

You can't remove a directory that contains files (a good safety precaution). To do so, you must change to the directory concerned, (with CD), delete the files and subdirectories in it (with DEL and RD), go back up one level and then remove the directory (with RD). Note that the same limitations apply to subdirectories as well; they must be empty before they can be removed, so you have to change to the subdirectory, delete all the files in it and go through the whole performance with each one of them.

Copying files

To copy a file from one drive to another, the COPY command is used. We will practice on FORMAT.EXE, with which we are already acquainted. Assuming you are logged on to a system drive, or the \DOS directory of your hard drive (use CD to get you there), put a formatted disk in the empty floppy drive and type:

```
COPY FORMAT.EXE A: (or B:)
```

If the file is present on the disk, you will see the disk access lights glow on the front of the drives as they are interrogated by the computer for information, and parts of the file are transferred a bit at a time.

Strictly speaking, you should include the drive letter and path with the source filename, but because you're copying from the current directory, you can safely leave it out (the computer knows where you are already). If you were copying the file from another directory, of course, you would have to include the drive letter in the command.

Now type:

```
DIR A: (or B:)
```

again, and you will see the file you just copied on the directory listing for drive B:. Note that you have *copied* the file, and not *moved* it – the original is still where it was (the MOVE command, if your version of DOS has it, will have the same effect as COPY, but the original will be deleted).

Practice

Copy several files to the other disk, one after the other, until you are happy with the concept of making duplicate files; about 10 should do it. In *Windows*, you would just open the *File Manager* program, select the directory you want to copy *from* and *drag* the files required to their destination.

Just to remind you, the command (in DOS) is:

```
COPY filename.ext B:
```

where *filename.ext* represents the name of the file you want to copy, including its extension (not all files use .EXE!). If you want a selection of files to choose from, list the files available on your current drive (the one shown at the prompt), with DIR. Don't forget that the full stop between the different parts of the filename is not shown on screen, but needs to be included in the command. So:

```
FORMAT    EXE
```

is equal to:

```
FORMAT.EXE
```

After you've copied a few files, check what's on the other disk again with DIR.

Wildcards

Copying files individually is all very well if you've only got a few of them, but the process can be tedious when there are lots. *Wildcards* can simplify the process.

In poker, a wildcard is one that stands for another card, like the ace, which can represent anything. In the computer world, the principle is the same, where a wildcard is a *symbol* that stands for a word or a letter. There are two of them, * or ?, respectively, so if you typed the command:

```
COPY *.EXE B:
```

you would copy every file with the extension .EXE to B:, regardless of what the first part of the filename is.

Similarly, if you typed:

```
COPY *.* B:
```

you would end up with *every* file, whatever the filename or extension is. Try both commands and see.

The other wildcard is the question mark (?), which stands for a single character only. It's not often used, but it does give you a handy way of dealing with filenames with spaces in, because although you can create such files (mostly by accident), you can't do anything else with them. Simply replace the space with ? and you can get DOS to recognise the file.

Copying disks

You will need to be able to copy disks for security purposes, and there are two ways of doing it. The long way round is to format another disk and copy the files from one to the other as described above but, even if you use wildcards, this can be time consuming. Alternatively, you can make exact duplicates of diskettes with the DISKCOPY command.

Unfortunately, there are disadvantages to this as well. For one thing, you get everything, and there may be some files you don't need.

A secondary reason is that you can't DISKCOPY with dissimilar sized disks, like a 3.5" in relation to a 5.25". The main one, however, concerns the computer's untidy housekeeping.

Imagine you've typed a report and and saved it. That report will occupy a certain amount of continuous space on the disk, which is OK when the disk is relatively empty.

Then you do other work and occupy the space surrounding your original report. If you subsequently re-edit that report (and make it longer in the process), the computer will find that it can't put the new edition in the original space. What it does then is to put the additional bit somewhere else on the disk, making a mental note of where it put it, because it's more difficult to move all the other files out of the way.

If lots of similar tag-ends are made, a single document could end up in dozens of different places with bits here and bits there, giving you a very untidy disk, which makes things run much slower than they need to because of the extra chasing around to find everything (this is known as *fragmentation*). You can either use a special program that puts it all together again (called a *Disk Optimiser*), or COPY the files to an empty disk which will make sure they're all joined up together in the right order.

However, serious fragmentation only occurs if you've been using the disk for some time.

Batch processing

In line with the tradition of getting the computer to do the work for you, batch files are used to simplify the way you give DOS instructions. A batch file is simply a list of commands that the system issues on your behalf—you collect them all together into one file, hence the name *batch*. If you like, they're the DOS version of macros.

> This way, you can save typing the same commands over and over again, and replace many of them with one. Batch files also reduce the chances of making mistakes, since the computer will be less forgetful than you are!
>
> Using batch files is like simple programming, and they can be as simple or complicated as you like. Create them with any *text editor* (see Appendix C) that produces *ASCII files*—a small example of a batch file is Z.BAT, which follows:
>
> ```
> @ECHO OFF
> cd\
> cls
> ```
>
> It's a useful routine for returning to the root directory and clearing the screen quickly—you only need to type <Z> (the name of the batch file) instead of the dozen or so keystrokes you would otherwise require. So that the computer knows the file contains a list of commands, the file is given a .BAT extension.
>
> The first line stops the commands cluttering up (or being *echoed to*) the screen as they are executed; the @ stops the line containing the words *Echo off* appearing, so you could place @ the beginning of every line if you wanted to, to get the same effect. Note that each command has its own line, with a Carriage Return and Line Feed at the end of it (press <Return> each time to produce a Carriage Return and Line Feed).
>
> Usually, commands are issued in the order they are given, that is, line after line, but there are ways of skipping bits of a batch file if they're not needed—see your DOS manual about the GOTO instruction and *labels*, if you're interested.
>
> The name of the batch file should not be the same as any .COM or .EXE files, because they will always take priority. You can *chain* batch files (that is, make them run one after the other) by using the name of the next as the last line of the previous one, but you must use the CALL command if you want to return to the original.

To save *environment space* (see Chapter 10), and reduce the length of the PATH statement (explained in Appendix A), make a batch file for each of your programs and put them all in a directory called \BAT. Then have that directory as the only one in the PATH.

Batch File Management

If you create large batch files, it can be impossible six months later to remember what the lines were for when you wrote them, so you can insert comments in your batch file as short notes to yourself. If you place the letters REM at the beginning of a line, that line will not be treated as a command, but as a REMark.

When testing, don't delete lines in batch files at random — it's best to disable them with REM, see what the effect is, then delete the line when you're happy. This is so that you don't forget what was there if what you tried doesn't work.

DOS Commands

There are many DOS commands available (just do a listing of the DOS directory), but you will be pleased to know you won't need to know all of them for daily use (about 18 is enough). Even those commands can be whittled down to the ones needed only when the computer is started, and about two or three that are used more often.

For example, one DOS command varies the keyboard's output according to what country you're in. It's called KEYB, which is short for KEYBoard, and you include a two-letter country code to tell it where you are. The command:

```
KEYB UK
```

therefore makes your keyboard behave like one in the UK.

Naturally, once you've loaded this program, you won't need it again while your computer is switched on, and you can safely ignore it. You can load commands like these automatically from a special batch file that is run only when the computer is started, called AUTO-EXEC.BAT, which is described in Chapter 10, *Setting Up Your Own System*.

Internal commands

Some commands are *built-in*, meaning that they are loaded into the computer's memory from the start and are therefore easily available (you won't see the names of these commands if you run the DIR command). Built-in commands are sometimes called *internal commands*. They include:

CD	Changes between directories.
CLS	Clears the screen.
COPY	Transfers files between devices (usually disk drives, but there's nothing to stop you copying to a printer or a screen).
DEL	Deletes files.
DIR	Gives the contents of the *current* directory, unless another is specified.
MD	Creates directories.
PATH	Establishes a permanent search path for files, usually from AUTOEXEC.BAT.
PROMPT	Modifies the prompt display on screen — again, usually from AUTOEXEC.BAT.
REN	Renames files.
RD	Removes directories.
TYPE	Lists a *text file's* contents on screen (the same as copying them to the screen).

Internal Batch commands

Some internal commands are usually used only in batch files:

@	Prevents a command from being displayed as it is run.
ECHO	Displays messages or command lines.
REM	Allows comments, or lines of text that are not treated as commands.

External commands

External commands are stored on disk until needed (if they were all loaded as internal commands, there would be no memory left for programs!). The most useful ones are:

DISKCOPY   Copies diskettes (of the same type).

FORMAT   Initializes disks so they can receive data — dangerous!

KEYB   Relates the keyboard to the language used.

XCOPY   An advanced form of COPY.

Stopping commands

If you need to stop a command once it has started, hold down the < Ctrl > key and press C (< Ctrl > -C) or the < Break > key (< Ctrl > -Break).

DOS Error Messages

Hopefully, you won't see too many of these, but there are one or two common ones that you need to know about.

Abort, Retry, Ignore, Fail?

This one most often occurs during a read or write operation when DOS can't carry on and wants to know what you want it to do about the situation, such as where you change to a disk drive and there's no disk in it, or a file being read has become corrupted. Simply type the first letter of the courses of action proposed, e.g. **A** for **Abort**.

Abort   Stops the current operation and puts you back where you started. This is a last resort, because you will lose all data entered or modified since the application started.

Retry   Makes another attempt to carry out the operation.

Ignore   This disregards the error condition and carries on to the next stage, but your data could be corrupted. *This is dangerous!*

Fail   Notes that there is an error, but the command is not aborted, giving you a chance to continue or terminate.

How do I . . . ?

This part of the chapter discusses some of the most common tasks that need to be performed with an operating system, and gives brief notes about how to do it. Again, many of them can be carried out with *File Manager* if you're using *Windows*. Full details about the commands mentioned will be found in the DOS (or Windows) manual, but some of the suggestions given will only apply to later versions of DOS, so if you have an earlier one, you may have to think again!

Get help

There isn't much with versions of DOS prior to 3.3, aside from the manuals.

With later versions, however, there are two ways of getting help. Type the name of the command you want help with at the prompt, followed by the command switch /? or /h, and you will see a screenful of text appear with the information you need, albeit cryptic.

Within application programs, press F1, which is generally accepted as being the Help key. Mostly, it will be *context-sensitive*, or geared to part of the program you are actually working in.

Manage my hard disk

There are two aspects to this. First of all, trying to find your way round such a large storage space and, secondly, trying to cram as much data as possible on to it.

The former operation is carried out with the aid of the PROMPT command (so you can tell where you are) and the MD, CD and RD commands (to Make Directories, Change Directories and Remove Directories respectively).

The latter uses software that hangs around in memory and compresses data as it's written to disk, and decompresses it when it's needed again. You can get around double your disk capacity in this way, but how much extra you get depends on the type of file being compressed (data files work better than program files).

When the hard disk is compressed, all the files on your disk are converted into one big file, which is treated as another disk drive, D: (the drive letters are allocated automatically). The drive letters are swapped round so your programs can't tell what's going on.

Alter drive letters

Use ASSIGN as a temporary way of exchanging drive letters. This is most useful when you try and install software that expects to be loaded from drive A, and your drive B is the only one that fits the disk size you have!

You can allocate drive letters to a directory path with SUBST, or use JOIN to make one drive appear as a subdirectory of another one.

Manage memory

If you have a 286 or a 386-type machine (including a 486) with more than 1Mb of memory, you can load DOS into what's called the *High Memory Area* (see Chapter 9, *Under The Hood*). This leaves more room available in *base memory* for programs to load into.

Software *device drivers* are used to make this happen; HIMEM.SYS in MS-DOS, and HIDOS.SYS in DR DOS.

Check for free memory

A simple check is done by CHKDSK, which will tell you what you want to know almost as an afterthought. However, MEM (supplied with later versions of DOS) is much more comprehensive and will sometimes even give you a picture of how your memory is allocated. Third party programs can be better, though.

Tell the computer where to find files

Include the path in the command when you load the program, or specify search paths beforehand with PATH (for program files) and APPEND (for data files) in AUTOEXEC.BAT.

Hunt for files

With DR DOS, use the TREE utility.

With MS-DOS, try the DIR command with the /S switch. You could also use ATTRIB which, although not built for this purpose, does give a listing of all the files it has to look at for its own reasons.

Transfer (copy) files

You can do this from device to device on the same computer (most commonly between disk drives) or between different computers. Use COPY or XCOPY for the first task, and a communications program at each end for the second (you will also need a specially wired *null modem* cable).

Copy *hidden file*s with XCOPY.

Compare files

Use COMP, which compares two copies of a file and tells you what the differences are.

Rename files

Use REN.

Delete files

Use DEL.

Delete filenames with spaces in them

DOS will accept filenames with spaces in them, but problems will arise when you try to refer to the file later, such as when you want to delete or copy it. The space is thought of as a *delimiter* by COMMAND.COM, so the letters either side of the space are read as separate commands in their own right; DOS will therefore think you're trying to delete two commands rather than one filename, and say something rude.

Use the question mark wildcard instead of the space, then DOS will recognise the file.

Protect files

From other people

Lock the computer away!

More seriously, it's possible to hide files from sight or just make them Read-Only (where you can *read from*, but not *write to*, them) using the ATTRIB command. A PASSWORD command (if available) may allow you to restrict access to individual files and complete directories.

From deletion

Use ATTRIB to mark the files as Read-Only or Hidden, and they will automatically be protected from deletion. Some versions of DOS have software permanently loaded that marks files for deletion rather than actually deleting them (up to available disk space), so you can recover them if you have to.

Although it doesn't stop you from deleting files by accident, the use of proper backup procedures will at least help you recover from a disaster.

If you manage to delete COMMAND.COM from the root directory of your hard disk (it's one of the system files), simply boot from a floppy disk *that has the same version of DOS on it* and COPY COMMAND.COM over to the hard disk from it.

See also *Create a System Disk*, below.

Recover deleted files

Use the UNDELETE command, or third party software.

Unformat a disk

You can only do this to one that has been *safe formatted* with special procedures, and with later versions of DOS at that, unless you use (very) specialised third party software.

Create a system disk

The DOS system files consist of two hidden ones, plus COM-MAND.COM. Without these, a disk is not bootable. However, the hidden files need to be in specific places on the disk, so just copying them will not do, even if you could make them visible with ATTRIB.

Use the SYS command to transfer system files properly to an empty disk, or use the /S switch when you FORMAT the disk.

Format a disk

Use the FORMAT command. If you want the system files transferred as well, use the /S switch with it.

Create batch files

Use a *text editor* (see Appendix C) to create a file with a .BAT extension. Make sure each command is on a separate line, and that each line ends with a Carriage Return and Line Feed (i.e. press < Return > at the end of each line).

Redirect output

You don't have to send your output to a file – you can send it to the screen or printer instead, for which the *piping* symbols > and | are used.

Display graphic characters on a CGA screen

Load GRAFTABL when you start your computer.

Stop a process happening

Use < Ctrl-C >.

Change the computer's method of operation

Use the MODE command to vary the way the screen works, or modify the speed of the serial ports and keyboard.

Get the best hard disk performance

- Defragment your files with a disk optimiser.

- Use a disk cache.

- Use buffers properly.

- Set the optimum disk interleave.

The last three are specialised; you will have to refer to Chapters 9 and 10 for background knowledge first.

Load a program automatically when the computer starts

Insert the command in AUTOEXEC.BAT.

Run several commands in one go

Create a batch file with the commands in it.

Get the right currency sign

On the screen:

- Use the right keyboard driver (load it from AUTO-EXEC.BAT). However, Windows has its own arrangements.

- Tell your application what country it's in (there should be a SETUP routine). Try *International* in the Windows *Control Panel*.

- Use the < Alt > key and type the ASCII number on the *number pad*.

On the printer:

- Make sure the printer's DIP switches sre set to reflect the language you require. Look in the printer's manual for *character sets* and set the switches as described.

Make a backup

A backup is a separate copy of the contents of your disks kept somewhere safe in case of disasters.

For many reasons, it's best to do a *file-by-file* backup rather than a *disk image*. File by file means that data files are copied one at a time, and therefore end up all in one piece and are easily found again. A disk image is like a photograph of a disk, which will be restored *exactly* as it's found; this can sometimes cause more problems than it solves. For example, when you restore a disk image to a different hard disk, as you may if you either change your equipment or have a disaster with your first, you might find that the restore process won't happen because the space allocation is different.

You will also get exactly what the last disk had, complete with bad sectors where they shouldn't be (you might even get previously good data over the new hard disk's bad sectors). *Bad sectors* are areas where recording can't happen because the recording surface isn't good enough.

A *full backup* means what it says. An *incremental backup* only operates on files that have been modified or created since the last time you backed up (the computer knows automatically which ones they are).

The accepted backup system is with a *tape streamer*, or even a duplicate hard disk (*mirrored* or *duplexed* – see Glossary). Such equipment is expensive, however, and with a little organisation you can get away with just using floppies.

If you think about it, the only data that will change from day to day is your work. There's no real point, aside from convenience, in backing up something that doesn't change all that much, like program files, which are only copied into memory as and when required, and not altered; if you make a note of your directory structure, you can always reinstall programs from their original disks, even if you have to buy the computer and software all over again (the need to backup doesn't always arise from system failures – your machine could get stolen).

Your data, however, is a different story, and this will be almost impossible to replace by any other means than restoring a backup copy.

Split your data up into separate *directories* (see this chapter) and keep a separate floppy for each one. When you feel the need, just use the XCOPY command (*not* BACKUP — see below) with the /S and /E switches (just in case you have subdirectories) and fill up the floppies (of course, you need to be aware of their capacities).

The advantage of using XCOPY (or even COPY) is that the data is still in a readable form, which it wouldn't be with BACKUP, so you can restore individual files if you need to. BACKUP compresses data so it can get more on to a disk, so it's not directly useable without a special RESTORE process. Also, BACKUP is very sensitive to DOS versions, although later copies seem to be able to cope much better, but it's generally best not to mix them.

Be careful about using only one set of media and using it over and over. It's possible that one day the data on your hard disk will be corrupted as you save it and you then proceed to overwrite the good backups. Always use one or two floppies in rotation and check what you've got on them.

A suggested system is to get three sets of whatever you propose to use and do a backup every day, using a different set each time, so the fourth backup overwrites the first and at any time you will always have three days' work in hand. Simply add more tapes or disks if you want to go back further than 3 days.

A better way, however, is to use 10 tapes and label them Mon, Tues, Wed, Thu, Fri1, Fri2, Fri3, Month1, Month2 and Month3.

Use the Mon-Fri1 tapes for the first week, and for the second week, but use Fri2 at the end instead. Similarly, for week three, use Fri3. On the fourth week, use Month1 on the Friday, and continue through the next two months using Month2 and Month3 in their respective places.

In this case, you will have a full backup for every day of the last week, full weekly backups for the last month, and a full monthly backup for the last three months.

What you actually do, however, is a commercial decision largely up to you, and must reflect the value of your data against the cost of losing (or replacing) it.

Some more tips:

- Keep at least one backup in deep storage; that is, a *really* safe place!

- Don't keep all your backups in one location; it defeats the object. If your office goes up in flames, so will the backups.

- Use 3.5" disks if possible, because they're harder to damage.

- Don't economise.

- Backup *now*.

Restore data

Having a backup copy of everything is no good if you can't restore it again. Once you've done your first backup (with any non-standard programs loaded), it's a good idea to practice restoring to make sure the system works.

In fact, most people only need to restore one file at any one time; it's quite rare to have to do a complete backup after a disaster, although obviously it does happen. Many people do complete backups when they just want to use the tape to transfer the contents of one hard disk to another, or just change the equipment in their machine.

Install a program

See *Installation*, on the next page.

Learn about Windows

Use the Tutorial supplied with the program (under the *Help....* menu).

Application Software

This is what actually does your work—the instructions that are loaded into memory that in turn control the Central Processor, to make the computer into a useful tool. You won't have to write the instructions yourself, unless you like programming; normally, you buy them already written, on floppy disks, transfer (that is, copy) them to your hard disk (if you have one) and load them into memory from there. Note the distinction— hard disk space is *not* the same as memory!

If your computer only has two floppy drives, you will need to take the System disk out first and replace it with a disk containing the program you wish to use. The second disk (B:) is usually reserved for a disk containing your work, or the data created by the program.

The following chapters concentrate on what application programs can do for you. As it happens, people use only 10% of the facilities provided by any program for 80% of the time, so you won't need to learn much to get productive very quickly.

At the end of each chapter (except *Accounts* and *Communications*), you will find various exercises, loosely based on RSA standard, to try with whatever you are using.

Basics

Application programs have standard terms you must know about. They include:

Installation   A program can install itself on the hard disk for you, in all the right places. Normally, you just place the first disk out of the packet in the floppy drive and tell DOS (or Windows) to start the INSTALL or SETUP program from there. Then you feed the disks in one by one as instructed.

Once your software's on the hard disk, you will be able to set it up the way you want it, by changing the screen colours, telling it what sort of printer it will be talking to, etc, etc. Sometimes, this is done from within the program itself as it installs, but there is often a separate program to do it for you.

Loading   Either starting the program itself, or the process of copying a previous edition of your work from disk into memory so it can be worked on. Sometimes, this may appear on a menu as *Open...* (a file)

Saving   The reverse of loading; recording a copy of the data in memory to disk for later use.

Save as..   Very often, you need to vary the characteristics of what you're working on, such as change its name, or save it in another place under the same name, which is what this function allows you to do.

Import   The same as loading, but with data produced by another type of program, which will be converted as loading takes place.

Export   The reverse of importing; saving data in the format used by another program.

Insert   When *Insert mode* is in force, any characters already on the screen are pushed aside to make way for new ones. It's turned on and off with the < Insert > key.

Sometimes this is a command supplied to insert another file (or picture) into the document you are working on.

Overtype   Sometimes called *typeover*, this is the opposite to *Insert*, where characters on the screen are overwritten by new ones typed at the keyboard. This is turned on and off with < Insert >.

Cut and   The process of moving data from one part
Paste   of a document to another, or even from one program to another. You *cut* the block you want to move from one area and *paste* it to another, but you must *highlight* it first by *marking* it up as a *block*.

Macros   A macro is a prerecorded list of instructions that are activated by pushing one key, so you only need to do the hard work once, when you work out what the instructions are in the first place. Thereafter, push the activation key(s) and the instructions are repeated. Different programs have different ways of providing macros, and they are not always interchangeable.

Hot keys   A combination of keys used to start a particular process, like a macro, but also used to activate memory-resident programs which lurk around in memory waiting to be used. Hot keys are called "hot" because they produce instant results.

Menus   Like those in a restaurant, lists of the services available from a program. First-level menus may lead to sub-menus which narrow your choices down even further, and so on. Sometimes, choices on menus will also display a short-cut key (or combination of keys) which will bypass the menu system and activate the command you want directly.

Print Preview   This shows you what your work will look like when it's printed *before* you print it, usually accessed by switching the screen into a special graphics mode.

Portrait   The orientation of a page, where the width is shorter than the length.

Landscape   The orientation of a page, where the width is longer than the length.

Chaining   Temporarily leaving one program to run another. The first program isn't shut down, but suspended, so this has security implications when several people are sharing a system and they are not normally allowed to use anything other than the first program; if chaining is allowed, they can leave programs and do what they shouldn't.

Undo	The ability to get out of trouble by reversing what you just did (usually re-inserting words you deleted by mistake). Often found in the *Edit....* menu, if there is one.
Quit	Leaving the program *properly*, which is a good discipline to get into. You must save your work to disk *before* you close your computer down, because data stored in memory is lost when power is switched off. This is done automatically when you quit the program properly, but obviously not if you switch the machine off first!

Exercises

The following three chapters contain exercises to help you use the software described in them properly.

The first step with each is to load your application. As with any program, you have to type its name at the command prompt, followed by the < Return > key (you may have to change to its directory first, or include the directory path in the command, all described in this chapter). If you're using Windows or another graphical interface, just select the picture representing your program, then press < Return >. If you're not sure what the program's name is, look in the manual that came with it, or do a listing of the directory contents, and take a note of all the files with .BAT, .EXE or .COM extensions. Then try them one by one till you get the one you want.

Obviously, a general book of this nature cannot deal with the specifics of every program available; it's not intended to replace the manuals, after all, but to give you enough information so that you can look in them for what you need.

However, the core facilities in each type are the same, and you will find that the general principles all hold true.

4

Wordprocessing

Wordprocessors are by far the most popular application used on personal computers. They are replacements for typewriters, and much easier to use anyway, because you don't even need to know how to type; two fingers will do!

Using a wordprocessor means you should never need to retype whole documents — the idea is to get everything right before you print it, and you can read and re-read everything on screen and change the words as often as you like until you're happy. The clever bit is being able to type everything in as you think about it and tidy it all up later (called *editing*). Having done all that, you can save your work (that is, record it on to a disk) and re-use it later.

The idea behind wordprocessing is simple; having opened a document, you simply place the cursor at the point you wish to enter text, and start typing. You can either use the arrow keys to position the cursor, or move the mouse and "click" the button, if you have one.

You won't see what you type appear immediately on the paper in your printer — instead, it's stored in the computer's memory and only printed when it's correct (the screen shows you what's in the memory at any time).

In general, wordprocessors have the following facilities:

WYSIWYG   The ability to see your work on the screen the same way as it will be printed. The initials stand for *What You See Is What You Get*, and are pronounced *Wizzywig*.

Although this is the ideal, it really depends on what you're printing. If it's *monospaced*, that is, `looks like what you get from the average typewriter`, WYSIWYG is easily obtained with text-based displays (that is, non-graphics), because the printed output will then match what's on the screen. *Monospaced* means that every letter takes up the same amount of space, regardless of its width. For example, the letter I is thinner than the letter M, but the same space is occupied by both.

However, *proportional spacing*, as it's called, allows letters to adopt their proper widths, therefore looking much more natural (like the letters on this page).

With wordprocessors that are being used on text-based displays, but printing proportionally, you will therefore only get an approximation of what's on screen. Real WYSIWYG is only possible with wordprocessors used on machines with a sophisticated graphics capability.

Word Wrap

This is where the number of words is compared against the length of the line so you don't have to keep remembering where the lines end (as you would on a typewriter). The computer knows how long the line is and, as you reach the end of the line, the text will automatically move to the next one. Usually, this will be whole words at a time but, if not, you will be able to adjust the *hyphenation settings*.

Because of *word wrap*, the program will assume that every time it encounters a Carriage Return (which you get when you press the < **Return** > key), it's the end of a paragraph, regardless of whether that paragraph consists of one word or several.

**Block moves
/Cut and paste**

You can move any amount of text, from a word to a number of paragraphs, from one part of a document to another.

Typically, you will *mark* the beginning of the block of text you wish to move, *mark* the end, *cut* the text between the marks, indicate where you want it moved to, and *paste* it in the new location.

With a mouse, you would place the cursor at the start of the block, hold the left button down and *drag* the cursor to the end of the block, where you let go of the button. The resulting *highlighted block* will look similar to this:

> **Note**
> The files in the preceding list were formatted to be printed on a Hewlett-Packard LaserJet Series II with a Microsoft Z1A cartridge. If you are using a different printer or cartridge, your system may not display certain fonts as they were originally formatted, and some lines may extend beyond the right edge of the screen. To make this document as easy to read as possible, try one or more of the

Centring

Any text, such as a heading or a title, can be automatically centred on the page. Place the cursor on the line you want centred, issue the command, and it's done.

Styles and Templates

A style is a format you apply to a paragraph, or even a complete document (when it becomes a *template*). For example, every time you want a heading, you can create a *heading style*, which could be bold characters of a particular size (like the one above).

Then you can apply the style to any paragraph, and it will appear in the style you have chosen. The style for this particular paragraph, for instance, is Times, 10-point, normal weight and indented 1 inch.

Another paragraph (like this) could be indented 2.5 inches, and use a different typeface.

You can enter your text any old how for speed, then apply styles to it that you created earlier to tidy it up.

After a while, you will accumulate a list of favourite paragraph styles which will be a real time-saver when laying out documents. The hardest work will be typing in the text; laying out afterwards will be very much simpler.

You can also apply styles to whole documents, which will be called *templates*; you can design a memo template for memos, one for reports, one for acknowledgements, and so on.

Then, you open a document based on that template, and the paragraph styles and text you want permanently in it will be there already.

If you can't find *templates* in your manual, the process will be to create the skeleton document, then open a new one and *insert* or *read-in* the skeleton document.

Font

Technically, a font is a variation of a typeface but, in the computer world, the word *font* has come to be synonymous with *typeface*. So the font (or typeface) on this page is Times Roman.

Alignment (or Justification)

The alignment of text on a page can be *left-aligned*, *right-aligned* or *justified* (although you could say left- and right justified as well). The alignment of a paragraph is relative to which side of it is straight.

For example, the paragraphs in this book are *fully justified*, where both sides are straight, and all of the lines are the same length, except possibly the last one.

This paragraph, however, is left-justified, or *ragged right*, where only the left side is parallel with the side of the page. You can see the lengths of the lines are not the same, and that the right margins don't line up.

This paragraph, of
course, is right-justi-
fied; the left margin is
not straight.

Spellchecking

A dictionary will help you check your spell-
ing, but it will only be able to proofread;
you won't be able to find the meanings of
words.

Thesaurus

The ability to get the wordprocessor to
suggest words and phrases when you're
stuck for inspiration.

Search and Replace

This is used for the obvious, like finding
and replacing phrases or words to save you
doing a lot of unnecessary typing to fix
mistakes. However, it can also be used
intentionally to improve productivity — for
instance, if you have a document where
long phrases are commonplace, you can
substitute one of these phrases with a symbol, say an asterisk (*), and use Search and
Replace to change it back when you're
finished, which saves you typing out the
long phrase so many times the first time
round.

It's also useful for converting ASCII files
to a particular wordprocessor format — see
Chapter 8.

Indexing

You will be able to get more powerful
wordprocessors to sort a selected number
of words into alphabetical order with the
page number they occur on. Some do this
automatically but, usually, you have to go
through the whole document and mark
every word you want to be in the index, and
have the wordprocessor compile it. Although sometimes this can be tedious, it's
still quicker than doing it the traditional
way.

Table of Contents   Similar to indexing, where the wordpro-
                          cessor takes all the headings in your text
                          (that is, those defined by paragraph styles)
                          and compiles them into a table of contents,
                          complete with page numbers.

Headers/Footers   These are lines of text that you want to
                          appear permanently at the top (head) or
                          bottom (foot) of your page. A page number
                          is a footer, but many people also include
                          the chapter title and other information.

Page formatting   You will be able to arrange your text to suit
                          your page size – that is, set top and bottom
                          margins, left and right, etc. *Page offset* is an
                          additional amount of margin over and
                          above the normal.

Mailmerge   The ability to merge a list of names and
                          addresses (or any details that vary, for that
                          matter) with standard text so that each
                          document looks individually prepared.
                          Typically used to create standard letters
                          with different names and addresses each
                          time.

The components of a mailmerge are:

● The *standard letter* you want to send.

● A *data file* with the names and addresses you want to send it to. This
must be in a particular format, usually
comma separated variable, or CSV
(see Chapter 5).

The standard letter has special symbols
representing the parts that will change,
e.g.:

```
&Name&
&Address1&
&Address2&
&Address3&
```

The items between the special symbols are known as *variables* (because they change), and their names must correspond to the names of the fields in the data file. The data file must contain the details required in the proper order; that is, as the standard letter expects to receive them.

When the mailmerge is run, the contents of the two files are combined until the data file is exhausted or you run out of paper.

Desk Top Publishing

This is related to wordprocessing, but you don't get the same sort of facilities. This is because DTP programs are actually *typesetting* programs, and meant to be used by professional printers and/or publishers. However, you will be able to do limited wordprocessing, to save you changing programs too often.

On the other hand, lots of wordprocessors have many desktop publishing capabilities; they may not be what a professional requires, but the output quality is as near as makes no difference to anyone else.

Merely having DTP software doesn't make you a professional typesetter — you must have a feel for what looks right, which is outside the scope of this book.

Wordprocessing Exercise

The remainder of this chapter is a practice session which you can use with your own wordprocessor. Don't forget that, when typing, paragraphs should have one clear line between them (you get a paragraph every time you press **< Return >** to start a new line, even if the paragraph only has one word). There should be one space:

- Between each word.

- After a comma.

- After a semi-colon.

- After a full stop.

- After an exclamation mark.

- After anything ending a sentence.

However, if you're using `monospaced text`, there are two spaces at the end of every sentence.

When you load up your wordprocessor, you may already be in an open document, and you will only be asked to give it a name when you come to save it (it's given a name so it doesn't get mistaken for another document). Some older programs, however, ask you straight away what document you want to open, and therefore need a name immediately.

As you will be creating a file, the name you give to this practice document must be less than eight characters long, and consist of only letters and numbers. The name should not be the same as any other document you may already have created, but most programs will automatically detect if you're trying to issue duplicate names and will ask you for another name if need be.

In any event, you will then be faced with the electronic equivalent of a blank sheet of paper, 25 lines long. At this point, you can go ahead and type what you want, and you will see the characters appear on the screen, inside the margins (the width of the margins can be changed to suit how you want your page laid out).

Use the text below to practice with, and type the next five paragraphs in directly, which will be altered as the exercises progress. You won't need to press **< Return >** at the end of each line; just let the computer calculate the length of it and place the characters on the next line for you.

The layout of text on your screen will not necessarily match that of the text on these pages; this will depend on your margin settings. At the end of each paragraph, press **< Return >** twice, so you get an empty line between each one.

Once you've finished the exercise, you will find the rest of the story at the end of the chapter!

1   Power up your computer and load your wordprocessor. This will be done by either typing the name of it at the DOS prompt, or selecting its icon if you have a graphic-based display, like *Windows*.

2   Type in the following text:

```
BOFFIN THE GNOME

Boffin the gnome lived in a computer. It was
his job to look after everything and make sure
that events ran smoothly - for instance, all
the little pixies that moved letters around
the screen and the elves that did the other
fetching and carrying came under his supervi-
sion, although they didn't actually see him
often. He usually let a friend of his look
after them most of the time.

Every computer has its own personal gnome in
charge of it, and the sort of computer it is,
together with the work it has to do, is de-
cided by the type of gnome it has. Some com-
puters draw pictures and some help in printing
books, so these will have an artistic or a
bookish type of gnome to look after them (Bof-
fin had a brother called Boris who lived in a
portable computer, so he was regarded as a bit
of a gnomad, although with Boffin around, he
always had a gnome to go to).

Boffin's computer was a large one, so he had
quite a bit of responsibility. It had a lot of
storage space where letters and numbers could
be held temporarily while they were being
worked on, and it was Boffin's job to look
after data and produce information when re-
quested.
```

```
Boffin, who was a scientific gnome by train-
ing, lived in a big black house in the centre
of the computer, the square one with the most
pillars holding it up (No 386). He didn't have
it all to himself, though, because he also had
several Senior Elves as lodgers whose job it
was to make decisions as to what to do with
the information that came their way (like many
other gnomes, he really lived in his office,
which was known locally as the Gnome Office).

At the back of Boffin's computer, where the
Big Red Switch was, there was a Power Station
which supplied different kinds of electricity
for the different houses inside - even back-
wards electricity. Some electricity was col-
oured, so it could be used on the screen for
pictures or lights on the front of the com-
puter.

Electricity was generated by naughty elves who
were made to run round and round in a giant
treadwheel (gnomes are never naughty).
```

At this stage, it's a good idea to save your work as a safety precaution. You will need to refer to your wordprocessor's manual for the correct procedure, but usually one of the function keys will do the job (try F10).

You will be altering the text from now on, so it's a good idea to open a new document with a different name, copy (or *read-in*) the document containing the above text into it and make the alterations to that. Alternatively, make a copy of the original and open it directly. That way, you will always have the original to fall back on if you find a mistake; otherwise you would either have to reverse all the changes (if you can work them out) or retype the whole document.

3   In the first paragraph, delete the words `, although they didn't actually see him often`

Place the cursor immediately to the left of the first letter to be deleted, then press the < Delete > key. Alternatively, place the cursor on the last letter, then use the < Backspace > key.

Although you could do this with each letter in turn, it's very tedious if you've got a lot of text to delete. A better method is to highlight the whole range to be deleted (as a block), then delete the lot in one go.

4   In the final paragraph, insert the words on the right hand
    side, before where the Big Red Switch

    Find the place where you want to insert the text, place the cursor
    there, and begin to type the words to be inserted. You should find
    that the words already there move over to make way for the new ones.
    If not, press the < Insert > key to go into *Insert* mode, and you will
    find it works.

5   Delete the paragraph beginning Boffin, who was a scien-
    tific

    Again, for wholesale destruction, delete each line at a time or
    highlight the complete paragraph and delete it all at once.

6   Add the following paragraphs after the fourth paragraph, which ends
    as the Gnome Office.

    There were several other houses around and
    about Boffin's house, and in each lived an-
    other gnome, also in charge of several elves
    who had a special job to do. For example, one
    of Boffin's friends, Adder, lived in the next
    house (no 387) and took care of all the mathe-
    matics. Another good friend was a lady called
    Dot Matrix, who ran the print shop. One of her
    machines never worked properly at all, so it
    was called a Lazy Printer.

    The gnomes who lived at 232, the railway sta-
    tion, were quite chaotic, and always left
    their house in a muddle, so that anyone send-
    ing information their way had to make sure
    that they sent it properly and at the right
    speed (all this double checking makes things
    run a lot slower than they should). The elf in
    charge there was called PIP.

    Go to the end of the fourth paragraph, press < Return > twice and
    commence typing the new ones.

7   Set in the whole document by half an inch at both the left- and
    right-hand margins.

    This means decrease the width of the available page by widening the
    margins.

Text-based word processors will have a screen 80 characters wide, with a density of 10 characters to the inch, so half an inch is the equivalent of 5 characters. If your page starts at column 1 and ends up at column 65, you would have to make the text start at column *6* (1 + 5) and end at column *60*.

However you do it, you should find the text will *reformat* automatically to the new settings. It's possible that you may have to *manually reformat*, which is something you will have to do on each paragraph affected.

You may have to use the *Page Setup....* routine of your wordprocessor, but if you're using *Windows*, just drag the margin markers to the place you want them (they look like square brackets, and are placed at either end of the ruler: [ ]).

8   Save your work, and print one copy with an *unjustified* right-hand margin.

This means that the *text alignment* should be *left-justified*. With most wordprocessors, this will be the norm, but yours might fool you and start up automatically creating fully justified paragraphs. *The text in this document isn't justified!* It's a trick question!

You will need to change the *paragraph style* to alter this permanently. Temporarily, just highlight the text and change it.

9   Set the document in *double line spacing* with *justified margins*.

Double line spacing inserts a clear line between every line. It's commonly used for draft copies of documents so there's plenty of space for people to make corrections and put rude comments in. To get the computer to do it for you, look under the *Format* heading in the manual and proceed from there. You should be able to set the justification from there as well.

Some more about Boffin

Just in case you're interested, here's some more of the story about Boffin . . .

Although the gnomes are in charge, all the running around is done by elves, and are in fact allowed to think for themselves once in a while (you will also find Goblins in a computer, but they're only allowed to make the tea).

Turning on the Big Red Switch gets the traffic lights running and sets several hundreds of elves scurrying about in all directions at once. It looks untidy, but actually every elf has a purpose and they're not allowed to run on anything other than the metal roads that connect all the houses together. Sometimes, the elves can catch the Data Bus, but this is nearly always late, because of the speed limits and the capacity of the roads between each part of the computer.

Because the road is so narrow, only a few buses at a time can use it, so they are always crammed with as many elves as possible, which is often counter-productive as the buses keep breaking down because of overloading.

The Local Bus is faster, but it only uses the wider roads near Boffin's house, so Elves have to change buses often if they want to move to different parts of the computer.

All the running around must also be done in strict timing, so everyone needs to be very fit. To make sure everything is done in order, there is a very large and expensive metrognome near Boffin's house.

During normal activity, some elves watch the keyboard for keys being pressed, others carry the letters (and numbers) required to the screen for the sprites and pixies to arrange, and then check back with Boffin's elves to make sure that those that appear are in fact the correct ones. In Boffin's computer, the pixies' chief was called WizzyWig, because he had a great shock of wild and woolly hair. It was up to him to make sure that what was on the screen actually ended up on paper. If the numbers are correct, Recording Elves make sure that the results are recorded on a magnetic disk, so that they can be called back and looked at later, a bit like you would with a video player.

Gnomes quickly learn to have a sense of humour, because elves are always getting up to mischief if they're not watched carefully, which to a gnome who is trained to think logically is not always a Good Thing — in fact, you could say it was bad for his 'elf! (Because of elves, Gnomes also learn very quickly to have good excuses ready in advance for when things don't go according to plan — they call this Elf Insurance.)

One day, things were proceeding smoothly enough when some bad elves, called Gremlins, managed to get in with nobody seeing them. Gremlins are well known to cause trouble with electrical things and, when something is not working properly without actually being inactive, you will usually find that a Gremlin is at the bottom of it.

Whereas elves are mischievous, and need to be carefully watched, nobody could ever accuse them of being nasty and vicious, so when they do get into trouble there is almost always a good feeling behind it all (the most punishment they ever get is a few days in the treadwheel in the powerhouse).

Gremlins, on the other hand, are different. They are nasty, vicious *and* 'orrible, and they don't care who knows it.

They look a lot like elves, but you can tell them apart because Gremlins carry large sticks called Mains Spikes, which they throw into machinery and poke Elves in tender places with when they aren't looking. Baby Gremlins are called Bugs, and cause just as much trouble, but they're so small you can't often find them.

Most days, Gremlins start off by upsetting the elves on keyboard duty. They lie in wait until one or two are rushing towards the screen and then ambush them, poke them with their Mains Spikes and steal the letters (or numbers) they are carrying. They leave those behind and carry their own to the Screen Reception Point. Their favourite trick is to add several noughts to other numbers, which means that people sometimes get paid far too much money.

Second favourite (but only because it's more difficult) is to mix letters and numbers up before they go to the printer or through the railway station.

Other well-known tricks include stopping everything working completely just when something interesting is happening (they do this with TVs as well) and making sure that nobody can find work where they put it. One particularly infuriating thing they do is put wrong numbers on the bottom of pages.

One day, Boffin was sleeping peacefully in his office when he was awakened by a commotion outside. Wondering what was going on, he got up from his bed and peeked out from between two of the pillars that held his roof up.

There was such a mixture of elves, fairies and pixies that you couldn't tell which was which, the way they were all jumbled together.

It looked as if a serious crash had taken place, as indeed it had, judging from what NickNick, the Traffic Police Gnome, had to say.

"What's happening?" asked Boffin.

"Mornin' Sir", replied NickNick, respectfully touching the brim of his helmet. "I'm afraid the traffic lights failed at this junction, Sir, just when everyone was coming to the same place rather fast and we've had two buses hit each other. We can't sort out the traffic properly just at the moment."

"Oh dear", said Boffin, rather absentmindedly, because he wasn't quite awake yet. "Can you do anything about it?"

"Not until some of those there back up a little", said NickNick, pointing to a small pile of smartly dressed gnomes who plainly weren't keen on moving anywhere.

It turned out that they belonged to Security, otherwise known as the Gnome Guard, and because they thought they were important, they considered they should have Right Of Way. As did the Elves and Pixies who were going the other way, of course.

The Gnome Guards' job is to make sure that only those elves allowed to go to certain places get there, and they give everyone passwords to make sure of it. Sometimes you can't even speak to a Gnome Guard unless you give them a password first! Although they aren't policemen, they like to think they are, which annoys NickNick and his colleagues, because they are real ones.

The security elves' leader was called Jobsworth. He secretly worked for the Chief Gremlin, whose name was Blitzen (he carried the biggest Mains Spike of all). He and his wife, Donna, were always fighting for the use of it. Between the two of them, there was very little to choose – they were both very nasty pieces of work.

Donna and Blitzen had a real speciality to upset computer users, which was to wait until they had been working for about ten minutes without saving anything, and then let fly with their Mains Spikes. This would upset the Elves' traffic flow so much that they would crash, which was what had just happened at the traffic lights (Jobsworth was lucky not to have got caught interfering with them as well). Then whoever was doing the work would have to start all over again, and make the Recording Elves work twice as hard.

Boffin sighed. Now he would have to go all the way through the Start Up procedure again. And it was beginning to be such a peaceful afternoon, too.

He told NickNick to spread the word and get everyone in their positions, and picked his way very carefully through the fallen bodies on his way to the Power Pack. He couldn't catch the Data Bus, of course, because the road was blocked, so he had to walk all the way, which did nothing to improve his temper.

When Boffin got there, he could see what had happened. There were several Gremlins crawling out from the wiring, wearing black and red striped jumpers with the sign of the Jolly Roger on them. Boffin sighed again. He knew what that meant — the dread Pirates were back in circulation, and since they weren't very hygienic (which means that they didn't wash too often) they'd brought all their germs with them, and no doubt had given 'flu and other viruses to all the elves in the power pack.

5

Databases

Databases contain information. So do the backs of envelopes, for that matter but, with them, you can't easily find specific details from the pile that gathers as your information grows. In your address book, though, you can quickly find a name by looking it up under the correct heading, using the name as a *key*. In other words, the information in your book is *organised*.

An address book is a familiar example of a database, with a telephone directory being but a larger version of the same thing. In them both, addresses and telephone numbers are related to names, which are *indexed* for ease of searching. Other examples could include spare parts catalogues, customer and supplier lists, personnel listings, etc, and you can probably think of many more.

The whole point of having a database in the first place is to *use* the information in it — data by itself is meaningless unless you can apply it to something. With databases, you put data in and get information out, and you could use that information to generate a mailmerge to only those of your clients in Australia who bought a particular product within a certain time period — and print all the labels!

Alternatively, it could be possible to obtain productivity or profit figures and keep track of how your company's performing.

There are two main reasons for having a database on a computer; one is to save time, and the other is to reduce the chances of error. Address books and telephone directories are OK if you want to find single entries, but imagine the time it would take if you wanted the names of all married people who have worked for your company for more than 10 years, over the age of 45; you would have to go through the whole lot at least three times to get what you wanted.

A database program knows how to store information and retrieve it, much as a librarian does with the books in a library, but it will search on the slimmest of clues and still find what you want. For example, you might file your doctor's details under "Doctor" in your address book, but that won't help anyone else who might be looking for the doctor's real name. With a computer database, that name can be found quickly, regardless of the classification it may be under.

Databases are very versatile, and the tasks they do can range from keeping a simple Christmas card list (and printing the labels!) to controlling the movement of stock round a warehouse.

Flat file databases behave like boxes full of cards, like those you find in the library. They are simple to use, but can be relatively slow in finding information and reporting on it. If you have one set of "cards" relating to customers and one to suppliers, and one person is common to both, that person's details will be kept in two places, taking up valuable disk space. Also, if anyone changes their address, you've got a lot of searching to do to amend your records.

A *Relational Database*, on the other hand, is able to relate different sources of information to each other, usually in the form of *tables*; one table could be full of names and addresses, whilst two others could relate to customers and suppliers, without their addresses, but with *pointers* to the address table, where they will be found (the pointer will typically be a code number given to a person).

The picture below illustrates this:

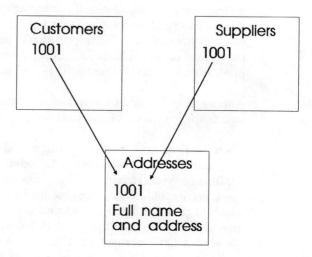

Disk space is saved because the addresses are only kept in one place, and the system is made more efficient because less searching is required.

A relational database will consist of a number of *tables* containing data, and queries (or reports) that extract data from those tables and present it in a meaningful way:

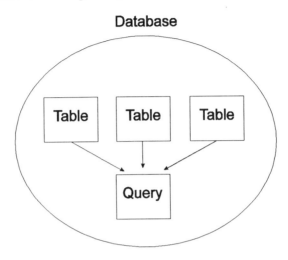

A query is just a specially generated table containing only the information you requested.

Common terms

All tables consist of the following items:

Field
An individual piece of information, such as a name, telephone number, part of an address, or whatever.

Record
A collection of fields relating to one subject, equivalent to a complete index card.

File
A collection of records, equal to the box containing the index cards. Depending on how your program uses its information, a *database file* may contain several tables, or be one constituent of a larger database.

The screen display will be different from the "card" or "file" layout; you will usually see a series of rows and columns in which the data is kept, in a similar manner to a spreadsheet. For example, your record card could look like the picture overleaf:

```
┌─────────────────────────────────────────────────────┐
│                  Record Card                          │
│                                                       │
│        Field1                                         │
│                                                       │
│        Field2                                         │
│                                                       │
│        Field3                                         │
│                                                       │
│                                                       │
└─────────────────────────────────────────────────────┘
```

But the corresponding screen could look like this:

```
                Field1        Field2        Field3

Record1
Record2
Record3
```

Each row in a database file (or table) contains a *record*, and each column contains a *field* within that record, so any record will have a number of fields related to it.

With information in them, therefore, your tables could look like this:

```
Name            Address             Telephone

Fred Smith      24 Acacia Rd        081 567 8907
John Smith      65 Acme Drive       081 676 8765
Jim Doe         51 Smith Rd         081 666 9978
```

Primary Keys

Each table must have one record as a *primary key*, so that records can be uniquely identified (it follows that you can't have duplicate entries in this one). You can use the primary key for *indexing* (or, in other words, use it as a basis for searches). You could index all the *name* fields in alphabetical order, for instance, and that will be the way the information will appear in any query you might run; the data on the disk won't change, but will be made to look that way by the index routine. You can have more than one key and, in some circumstances, it could be useful to index on all fields.

Primary keys are also used for creating relationships between tables; two tables can be related if the contents of the primary key in one table are somewhere in the other.

Planning a database

Whatever type of database you use, you must first decide what you want to get out of it, and hence what you need to put into it. For example, if you were running a video shop, it might be helpful to know not only what videos you have in stock, but how many copies of each title there are, and which ones earn the most money. On top of that, you will need to know which customers have them out on hire, how much is owed (based on what the nightly rate is), and the customer's telephone number in case they're late bringing the videos back. You would also need the address so you know where to send the boys round.

You need to think about splitting your data into tables and how to make them relate to each other, including making sure that different parts of the database aren't duplicated. In a large company, almost every division will use employee names and addresses, and it makes sense to stop them creating the same information more than once. Across the Company, therefore, it could be possible for all departments to use the personnel records.

How you structure records is important; for example, it's best to have peoples' names split into First Name, Second Name and Middle Initial, and the parts placed into separate fields. This automatically gives you a choice of three key fields, should you decide to use them for indexing, and problems will be reduced when transferring the data to another type of program; you won't have to worry about splitting fields up (split fields can always be combined for printing or displaying, anyway).

Creating a database

Having decided which tables will contain what information, you have to create the fields you want in each table, *before* you put the data in, so that the program knows how to classify your information.

You will usually need to supply a *field name*, together with its length and type. The name is used merely to identify the field from others, so that there's no confusion. The *length* concerns the amount of characters that the field is expected to contain. The *type* of field determines what operations can be carried out on it; for example, if they contain numbers, you can calculate on them, and text fields can be sorted alphabetically.

Types of field available

You can specify what type of data goes into a field, which is useful if other people put data in, because you can make the computer beep if it's wrong (known as *validating*). Types of field available include:

Character	Used for text, including telephone numbers, etc., which lessens the chance of them being treated as real numbers and included in calculations by mistake.
	Character fields can contain letters and numbers, and are left-aligned.
Numerical	These speak for themselves, but be wary of creating any with decimal places unless you have a maths co-processor.
	Obviously, if you want to use decimals, the system will work, but co-processors are specially built to cope with them; without one, decimals are converted to whole numbers, calculated upon, and then converted back again. Not good for performance!
	Numerical fields contain numbers, signs and decimal points and are right-aligned. If you designate a field as being numeric, you will automatically be asked how many decimal places you want.
Date	Databases (and spreadsheets) can calculate on dates; the date is reduced to a number, whatever its appearance may be on screen, which you can multiply, add subtract, or whatever. This type of field is eight characters long.
Logical	Logical fields allow for choice, like True or False (Yes/No), and have one character.
Memo	A field which holds any type of information, typically short notes, or anything else unstructured. Because of the nature of the data inside them, their contents are not usually displayed, although the presence of the field itself is indicated.

Setting up relationships

After deciding on the field structure in each table, the next task is to get them to work together or, in other words, create relationships between them. There needs to be at least one common field (that is, with the same value, if not the same name) in each of the tables to be related. Usually, this will be the *primary key*.

In the example below, the customer code is common to all tables; the name of the field doesn't need to be the same, just the contents.

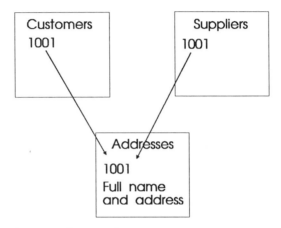

Relationships come in many forms:

- *One-to-many*, where one record in the first table will relate to several in another; for example, you could have customer and order tables, and there could be more than one order per customer, but only one customer per order.

- *One-to-one*, where one record in the first table will relate directly to one in another. There's not a lot of point to this, as you could simply merge the two tables and make life simpler.

- *Many-to-Many*, where tables can have more than one matching record in others.

Looking at your data

You may need to search for a specific item, or several that nearly match, either because you want to change something, or you genuinely want information. You will be able to view your records on screen, and move forwards or backwards between them in three ways:

- As a *table*, where you look at them all at once, in a list. In other words, you can *browse* through them at your leisure (BROWSE is a commonly used database command). Unfortunately, you can't do much else whilst browsing, and you usually want to look for a specific item, anyway.

- As a *form*, where a predetermined arrangement is used to display one record at a time, just like you would see it if it were printed on paper. Forms are sometimes designed with a *screen builder*, and you can specify how data will be displayed in each field (for instance, you might like the date displayed as numbers rather than text).

- As a *query*, which will get particular information out. A query can use several tables and combine the answers into a temporary table as the solution to your problem. A query can be saved for re-use later, and you tell it what data you want from the tables with *search criteria*, such as numbers "greater than 60", "names equal to Jones" or "rating = PG". Special symbols are used as shorthand to help with this. They include:

=	Equal to
<	Less than
>	Greater than
>=	Greater than or equal to
<=	Less than or equal to
<>	Not equal to

- As a *report* which, at rock bottom, is nothing more than a query that is produced on paper.

Data exchange

You can exchange information between different types of database program, because a standard has emerged based on the original *DBase* format. Data files are structured in a certain way and usually have a .DBF extension to prove it.

Standards used

CSV Fields are separated by commas, and surrounded by inverted commas (if you have spaces in them that could be mistaken for delimiters, although some programs seem to be quite happy without them). The initials stand for *Comma Separated Variable*, and a line in a .CSV file could look like this:

```
"Fred Bloggs","29 Acacia Avenue","ANYTOWN"
```

TAB As above, but tabs replace commas. Also known as a *fixed length field file*.

ASCII A standard format, originally established to ensure printing is consistent between countries, but can also be used for data exchange.

Importing data

The data to be imported must be in the field order that your database expects; either get the exporting program to put it in that order, or sort them on the fly as you load them.

You can find out the order expected by filling in *every* field and printing the result. The fields on paper will be in the field order desired.

Database Exercise

1 Power up your computer and load your database program. This will be done by either typing the name of it at the DOS prompt, or selecting its icon if you have a graphic-based display, like *Windows*.

2 Create a database containing details about videos in a shop:

```
VIDEO NUMBER
VIDEO TITLE
COPIES
CLASS
TYPE
```

Class refers to censorship; whether 15, 18, PG, etc. *Type* refers to drama, comedy, thriller, etc.

Open a new database and tell it what fields you want included; here you want 5, and you will need to supply:

- The name of each field.

- Its length.

- Its type (e.g. character, numeric, etc).

Only *Copies* needs to be Numeric, because your stock numbers will need to be added up. The remainder can be Character fields.

If your database is Windows-based, use the *File* menu and select *New...* Otherwise, the most common command is CREATE, or something similar, together with the name of the database.

Save the database structure.

3 Enter the following data into your new database:

No	Title	Copies	Type	Class
1	Robin Hood	6	Adventure	PG
2	Ghost	7	Romance	15
3	Terminator	3	Thriller	18
4	Aliens	4	SF	18

Having created your database, you will need to use it, so you would issue the command USE, plus the name you gave it.

Adding records is usually done with a command like APPEND.

4   Alter *Terminator* and *Aliens* to read **PG**.

5   Delete videos with *Class* = **15.**

6   Add the following records:

No	Title	Copies	Type	Hired
28	Terminator II			

7   Sort the complete file in alphabetical order by TITLE.

8   Search the file for all titles of **PG** classification.

Open a query and tell it what fields are relevant to your search (in this case, *Title* and *Class*). Try looking for a LIST command and use it with FOR, e.g:

```
LIST FOR TITLES=PG.
```

9   Search the file for all titles classified as 15 with more than 3 copies, and print only the Number and Title.

6

Spreadsheets

A spreadsheet is a program that displays a screen divided into a series of rows and columns, like pigeonholes at a Postal Sorting Office, although you can't usually see the lines on screen (you have to imagine those). The boxes created by the rows and columns are called *cells*, which are referred to by row and column; e.g. B5, below:

	A	B	C	D	E	F
1						
2						
3						
4						
5		[ ]				
6						
7						
8						
9						
10						
11						
12						
13						
14						
15						

It's like using a giant piece of graph or ledger paper, but you will also notice the similarity with browsing a database table. Because of this, spreadsheets can be used as databases, provided they can handle dates and text as well as numbers, but only up to a certain point, because they are not meant for handling large amounts of data (on average, the maximum is about 8,000 records).

Spreadsheets can be thought of as advanced calculators and, for most applications, including accounts, will be more than adequate for most peoples' needs. They are programmable (that is, you can use macros and get them to make decisions), they can sort information into any order you want (like a database) and they can even be used as a wordprocessor, since they accept text as well. Although limited in this respect, they are still great for producing standard letters with the results of your calculations.

You can also create graphs from your data, do statistical calculations and get it to show you what would happen if, say, you reduced your prices by 10% or made 20% more profit. This is done by creating a *mathematical model* of your business that shows where the money is coming from and going to, so you can immediately see the effects of a price rise in any particular area.

One particularly useful facility is *back solving*, which works backwards from a result. For example, instead of calculating profit from income, you can also get the spreadsheet to calculate what income would be required to get a specific profit.

Cells are numbered by rows, and typically lettered by column, so you start at A1 and end up in something like ZZ9999, depending on how large your spreadsheet is. Naturally, you can't fit all the cells into a single screen, so you use the screen as a *window* (or magnifying glass) to pan over the rest by using the cursor movement keys or your mouse.

If you find it difficult to wrap your brain round column letters and row numbers (B1, Q2, etc), you can always give names to cells, or collections of cells, which are called *ranges*, so you can refer to them more easily. It's easier to say SUM SALARIES rather than SUM A1..A244!

There are three types of cell contents; text, numbers and formulae.

Text   This is used mainly for headings, so you can describe what the numbers mean, but is also useful if you want to enter figures that shouldn't be calculated upon, like telephone numbers and dates (spreadsheets generally tend to ignore leading zeros and suppress them, which will make nonsense of your telephone directory).

Text in a cell is referred to as a *label*, and will use one or two special symbols to vary its appearance in the cell.

'   Left aligned

"   Right aligned

^   Centred

\   Repeated across the cell

Numbers

Numbers speak for themselves, really. If you don't specify that a number is to be treated as text, (by using any of the above symbols first) it will be automatically be right-justified in the cell.

Formulae

These are the real reason for using a spreadsheet. That is, instead of text or numbers, you can insert a calculation into a cell, and the spreadsheet will do your sum for you. You won't see the formula in the cell, but the results of the calculation.

Common symbols used in formulae are:

=   Equals

+   Addition

*   Multiplication

-          Subtraction and negative values.

/   Division

%   Percentage

.   Decimal point

()   Brackets (a subset of a calculation).

@   The @ sign tells the spreadsheet to run a *built-in function*, or one it's already programmed to do, so you don't have to remember tl e keystrokes. For example, ()SUM will give you a total of a range of cells, or @AVG will give you the average.

So you don't confuse the spreadsheet, a formula is started with a maths symbol (usually +, but @ if you're using a built-in function. Sometimes, though, it could be =). This is so the formula is not mistaken for text or numbers; for example, to add the contents of three cells, you could use:

```
+B1+B3+B5
```

To save keystrokes, if you're calculating over a range of cells, use a double dot (..) or a colon (:) between the start and end cell numbers of the range, and enclose the whole lot in brackets (this is described more fully later, but the range above would look like B1..B5).

Example

Imagine a small decorating business that has been asked to quote for the decoration of a small house with three rooms.

On paper, you could write down brief details somewhat like this:

```
Paint        30
Wallpaper    50
Labour       60
Total       140
```

You could insert the same figures into a spreadsheet, but if you had to add up the figures and work out the total yourself, there would be no point so, with a spreadsheet, the total *140* can be replaced with a formula, such as:

```
A       B            C

1       Paint        60
2       Wallpaper    50
3       Labour       60
4
5       Total        +C1+C2+C3
```

This would result in the same figures (140) being shown in C5, but if you had to change the contents of any cells affected by the formula (C1, C2 or C3), the total would change automatically (to 170, in this case).

The formula used above, +C1+C2+C3, is OK for one or two cells, but would become unwieldy if you had to calculate through 24! This is where the @ function comes in, and you can replace the above formula with:

@SUM(C1..C3)

which is much more elegant.

With the formula, you are invoking the built-in SUM function with @, and instructing the spreadsheet to SUM the range of cells beginning with C1 and ending with C3.

Macros

Macros are pre-recorded instructions that are replayed by pressing a simpler key combination. This not only saves you repetitive typing – the computer is faster and makes fewer mistakes!

Note that macro instructions are stored *inside the spreadsheet itself* in their own range of cells. You then *name the range* with a single letter, and invoke the macro by pressing < Alt > plus that letter, although the activation key will change from program to program.

Macros in spreadsheets are most useful for those little tasks you do often, like inserting and deleting rows and columns, that take quite a few (and sometimes awkward) keystrokes.

Print macros are the most common, because you always have to nominate the range of cells you want to print, plus a few other instructions, but you can automate almost any process, even creating a complete menu system so that others can use your spreadsheet without doing any damage.

Macros are also useful for recreating keystrokes that you may have got used to in other programs.

Presentation

Having all this data is no good unless you can present it properly. Changing the way your spreadsheet looks is called *formatting* (nothing to do with disks), and you can make your work prettier or more relevant to your circumstances. For example, you can designate cells as being in *currency format* (which automatically include a currency sign), widen columns to fit your text, etc, etc.

You get to such facilities through a menu system which will usually be invoked with the forward slash key (/), unless you're using a mouse, in which case you can choose them in the normal manner.

Productivity tips

Number One is.... *don't* experiment before saving your work – this specially applies to macros and printing.

Organisation

There's no reason why you can't combine several small spreadsheets on one large one, especially if their results depend on each other.

However, if you have to expand a sub-spreadsheet (e.g. when adding macros), the chances are that an adjacent one will also be interfered with, so the trick is to add them in blocks diagonally (as shown):

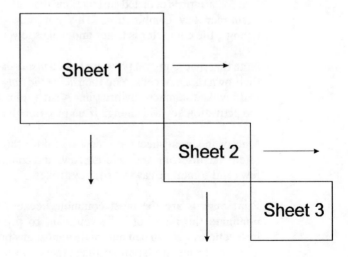

Place lines around each block and *name each one* to make identification easier. Press the GoTo function key (F5 usually) followed by the Name key (F3) and you will be taken precisely where you want to go to. The impression will be moving from page to page rather than around one large spreadsheet.

Many spreadsheets allow you to place one sheet on top of another, rather like in a notebook, to get the same effect.

Templates

Once you've created a spreadsheet, think about whether you're going to use it again. If so, make it into a standard model (sometimes called a *template*) which is nothing more than the spreadsheet structure without the data, which can subsequently be inserted as and when required.

Printing

This is often difficult with a spreadsheet, although the better ones have the ability to calculate what size the print needs to be to get on one page (you have to get your own magnifying glass, though!).

Printers have a *condensed type* facility which allows you to get more characters on to a page, but you might find yourself having to print sideways, since most spreadsheets have more columns than rows. If you have to print in *landscape format*, make sure you tell the spreadsheet that the columns are wider and that the page is shorter, say 132 by 50.

Macros

You can create an empty spreadsheet that contains nothing but macros. Some spreadsheets allow you to keep a library of macros, so designate the one with the macros as your library. If you load it automatically when the program starts, you can then use the macros from any spreadsheet.

Data entry

You don't need to press **< Return >** plus the arrow key to go to the next cell — enter your text and press the Arrow directly.

If you have a lot of data, it's often quicker to enter it into a wordprocessor, and save it as a .CSV file (*comma separated variable* — see also *Databases*). This means that you will have to place a comma between each cell entry, and surround the entry with inverted commas if it's intended to be text (and has spaces in it that could be mistaken for delimiters).

Once you import the file, each line of it will occupy a row, and each comma-separated field will ocupy a column within that row.

Totals

For minimum scrolling, consider putting your column totals at the *top* of the column, rather than at the bottom, as you might if you used a sheet of paper. This allows you to keep your values in view, especially if you *lock* the rows (that is, make sure they don't move relative to the other cells).

Sorting

Any column or row can be sorted into ascending or descending order, but if you sort one column, related information in other columns won't automatically change in line with it.

You must highlight the whole range relevant to the sort, including all columns and rows, and indicate which one you want the sort based on (you only need to select one representative cell from the column you want sorted), otherwise known as providing *search criteria*. All the data in the columns highlighted will move at the same time.

Other uses

Spreadsheets are useful for other purposes, but you must remember that these are adaptations – the job will certainly be done better with dedicated software. Having said that, if your need is only occasional you may well find that a spreadsheet is powerful enough and save yourself some money.

Databases

Spreadsheets can be used as databases, which is hardly surprising, considering the similarity in the use of tables. Columns can be sorted alphabetically or numerically, and information analysed according to your heart's desire.

However, spreadsheets store data in memory, which gives the illusion of speed, whereas databases keep data on disk for safety reasons. You therefore need to save your work regularly.

Graphics/Artwork

This makes use of the graph and presentation facilities of a spreadsheet. Make each cell into a very small square by reducing the width of the rows and columns and treat the result as a grid on which to draw your pictures.

Wordprocessors

All you need do here is make the first column (A1) as wide as your intended piece of paper, and treat the rows as lines (make the spacing 6 lines to an inch). It sounds easy, and it is; a spreadsheet has text editing facilities and can format text into paragraphs of any width, search and replace, move text, and also do many other things a wordprocessor can do.

Spreadsheet Exercise

This exercise calculates the expenses of a small company over six months. You will create a spreadsheet, enter numbers (and text describing them), insert and delete columns and rows, and copy formulae from one place to another. During the exercise, various short cuts common to all spreadsheets will be discussed.

1   Power up your computer and load your spreadsheet. This will be done by either typing the name of it at the DOS prompt, or selecting its icon if you have a graphic-based display, like *Windows*.

2   Enter the heading COMPANY EXPENSES.

The heading can be placed anywhere you like (it's your spreadsheet) but, usually, it's at the top left, so move the cursor, which indicates the active cell, to the top left hand corner of the spreadsheet, using the arrow keys, or click on the cell you want with your mouse. Cell A2 is suggested, as it's a good practice to leave A1 empty. This is because the < Home > key is used as a short cut to place the cursor into A1 instantly. If you include the < Home > key in a calculation or a macro, it's possible to damage the contents of A1, so it's best to leave it alone.

The text you enter will be seen on the *input line*, which is normally at the top of the screen. Only after you've pressed < Return > (having finished typing) will what you've typed go into the cell.

Your screen display so far should look like this:

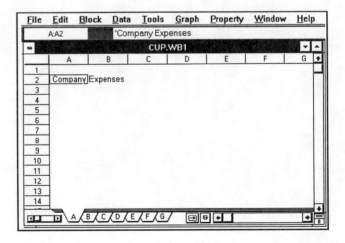

In this case, you will notice that the letters overrun the column width (which is normally 9 spaces or so). You could increase the column width at this point, but that may spoil it for other text in column A which we shall insert later. As you don't intend to have any text in the column to the right of A2 (B), you will see all of the words COMPANY EXPENSES as they overrun. As soon as you place any text in B2, however, the words COMPANY EXPENSES will be shortened (try it if you like). In this case, you will need to widen column A.

3   Starting in the first column, enter the following titles, representing the months of income:

```
Item Jan Feb Mar Apr May Jun Total.
```

Leave a spare line underneath the heading (that is, don't put anything in row 3), because it makes things look neater. Proper layout counts for a lot when it comes to readability.

Obviously, month names vary in length, so you may need to widen some columns to accommodate the text (check your spreadsheet's manual for how to do this).

This should be the result:

4   In the first column, enter the following areas of income:

```
Petrol
Parking
Office Equipment
Office Rent
Heat, Light, etc
Telephone
Postage

Total
```

Again, leave a space underneath the titles, to make it easier to read. You will need to widen the column to accommodate the length of some of the income areas.

Does it look like this?

A:A15								
				CUP.WB1				
	A	B	C	D	E	F	G	H
1								
2	Company Expenses							
3								
4	Item	Jan	Feb	Mar	Apr	May	Jun	Total
5								
6	Petrol							
7	Parking							
8	Office Equipment							
9	Office Rent							
10	Heat, Light, etc							
11	Telephone							
12	Postage							
13								
14	Total							

5   Now enter data under the following headings:

```
Item   Jan  Feb  Mar  Apr  May  Jun  Total

Petrol       25   36   47   23   33   25
```

You could place the numbers in, press **< Return >** then use the right arrow key to get to the next cell, but you will find it easier just to press the right arrow key and the numbers will be entered automatically. Notice that numbers are right-aligned inside a cell, whereas text is left-aligned. This is standard practice, to make it easier to tell them apart. You can change the alignment of text by placing any of the following symbols in front of the text as you enter it:

'   Left aligned

^   Centred

"   Right-aligned

The apostrophe is automatically entered, as text is left aligned by default.

6   Now carry on with the following:

```
Parking          12  12  13  14  22  18
Office Eqpt      102 34  68  66  45  38
Office Rent      33  33  33  33  33  33
Heat, etc        22  23  33  24  33  21
Telephone        104     107
Postage          24  34  25  26  27  28

Total
```

7   Save your work.

8   Change the *Office Equipment* figure for Feb to 48 and the Telephone figure for May to 99. Also, make the March *Telephone* figure 45.

9   Delete the *Office Rent* row.

10   Use a formula to calculate the totals for each month; that is, complete the entries for the *Total* row.

The formula could be something as simple as $+B6+B7$, etc, but this is only suitable for one or two entries. If you have twenty or so cells to work on, your formulae will get out of hand. Spreadsheets have built-in functions that can do the work for you, in this case @SUM (the @ sign tells the spreadsheet to use one of these functions).

@SUM is not the only one; you could have @AVG (for averages) or maybe @TODAY (for today's date).

In this case, use:

```
@SUM(B6..B10)
```

The figures inside the brackets represent the range of cells you want SUM to operate over. You mention the start cell and the end cell, and place a pair of dots in between to represent the cells in the middle (your spreadsheet may use a colon instead).

Having completed the first column's total, you now have to complete the others. Again, if you only had one or two to do, you could simply retype the formula and change the numbers as required, but you can simplify matters by copying the first cell's contents to the others in the row.

Place the cursor over the first cell, or the one you want to copy *from* (B13), and issue the command to COPY (you will have to check your spreadsheet's manual, but try /C or ^C. The forward slash is the most common way of getting a menu of commands with which to massage your figures.

Then place the cursor over the cell you want to copy *to* (C13), press <Return>, and you will see the totals appear there. Look at the input line, and you will see that the cell range inside the brackets has automatically changed to reflect the copying. The spreadsheet is smart enough to understand this sort of thing.

Again, there's a lot of typing involved if you were to repeat that process over a series of cells, so the trick is to copy over a *range* of cells.

To repeat the above over the remaining cells in the *Total* row, place the cursor over the cell you want to copy *from* (C13), issue the COPY command, and place the cursor over the first cell of the range you want to copy *to* (C14). So far the procedure is the same, but if you now press the full stop and use the arrow keys to cover the rest of the range (to G13), you will see the cells in that range being highlighted. Alternatively, use the mouse to highlight the range.

If your spreadsheet doesn't understand using the full stop to anchor the start of a range, try the F8 key or look in the manual for *extended mode*.

When you've finished, press <Return> and you will see your totals appear in the cells in the *Total* row. Check the input line to see if the numbers are correct; they will be.

11   Now use a formula to calculate the Total *column*. Simply repeat the copying process described above.

12   Insert a row before the *Telephone* row and enter the following data (don't include the column headings):

Item	Jan	Feb	Mar	Apr	May	Jun
Stationery	25	24	32	45	32	33

13   If you need to, recalculate the cells in the *Total* row and the *Total* column. You will probably be OK for the *Total* row, as the range numbers will have accommodated your extra row, but the *Stationery* cell in the *Total column* will be empty as you won't have placed a formula in there. Copy one from any cell in that column into it and you will see the total at the bottom change to the correct figure.

14   Just for the exercise, calculate the average for every row and place it in the column to the right of *Total*. This is simple enough; just use the same type of formula as you've used before, but replace @SUM with @AVG. Another way would be to take the contents of the total cell and divide it by the number of columns in the total, in this case 6, so your formula would look like:

      +H5/6

The plus sign is there to signify that the contents of the cell will be a formula, and not text or numbers. Sometimes an equals sign is used for the same purpose.

15   Now format the monthly cells as *currency cells*. This is a standard facility, where the figures will have two decimal places and the currency symbol for your country placed in front of them. Try looking under *Format*.......

16   Print your spreadsheet. You will have to define a range of cells for this first.

If you want your data to be printed sideways, which doesn't matter for this spreadsheet, but may do later, tell the software to print on Landscape format, and increase the number of columns available, while reducing the number of lines; try 135 columns by 60 lines.

7

Accounts

Accounts software is mostly written for accountants, who are trained professionals, and accordingly use the computer to take the drudgery out of their work. You must therefore learn accountants' language (as if computer jargon wasn't enough!) in order to use it to the best effect. Having said that, it can automate many procedures for you, such as updating several balances at the same time, rather than having you adjust them one after the other, as you would in a manual system (assuming you could remember which ones to do!), so this is not the problem you might expect it to be.

However, there are still some occasions where you do need to know your way around the books in order to get the results you want. For example, a credit note will often need to be physically matched against the invoice to which it relates.

Accounting Basics

Accounts work on the principle that, in the long run, you can't spend what you don't earn; in other words, what goes out is balanced by what comes in. As there are two sets of figures that must balance, the system used is called *Double Entry*. Luckily, you don't really need to get involved with this as many of the "double" entries are done for you (you won't actually have to make two entries for every transaction; the software will make corresponding balancing entries for every entry you make in an account).

Double Entry ensures that mistakes are easily detected. In any particular account, if the figures in the Out column don't match those in the In column, the totals at the bottom won't equalise, which means there's a mistake somewhere. The system is therefore self-correcting; if money moves into an account, it must move out of another, and that movement will be noted twice, either as a debit or a credit, depending on the direction of movement.

When you get more in than you spend, you have a *credit account*; where the money goes the other way, it's a *debit account*.

Traditionally, debits are recorded on the left hand side of an accounts page, and credits on the right, and this will be reflected in the printouts you get from your computer.

A company's accounts are calculated over a year, known as the *fiscal year*. Usually, this will coincide with a calendar year, but there are certain tax advantages to starting earlier than this – you don't get to pay less tax, but you do get to pay it later.

Daybooks (journals)

Daybooks, or journals (*jour* is French for day), are used to record daily transactions, the summaries of which are used to update *ledgers*. The process of updating ledgers is called *posting*.

You need a journal when you transfer amounts between *nominal accounts*. This is because the double entry system needs the details recorded twice for every transaction. The journal entries therefore serve as a halfway house; for example, you put cash into a cash account, which then needs to be transferred to the Bank account. To reduce the balance on the Cash account, cash needs to be transferred to the current account via a journal.

Ledgers

Whereas journals *record* information, ledgers *classify* it. A summary of each journal is transferred to a *ledger* so that it's easy to add up the balances without going through every entry in the journals.

Sales and Purchase Ledgers

These perform similar functions, the only difference being that one deals with what you sell and the other with what you buy. They are easily dealt with together.

The *Sales Ledger* keeps track of invoices issued and cash received, and therefore can tell you the people who haven't paid their bills yet (that is, your *aged debtors*). Note that the software can only do this if you give it the information it requires – having issued an invoice, you must then input the details of any cheques or payments received against them, so that the balances are cleared. Any balances not cleared belong to your debtors, and you can send them statements to hurry things up (or get the computer to do it). Depending on your software, this process can be automated as well.

Unpaid invoices can normally be identified for 30-day periods, e.g. 30, 60, 90 and over 90 days.

A similar process happens with the *Purchase Ledger*. When one of your suppliers sends you a bill, you tell the computer about it, as you do when you pay up. At the end of the month, or whatever, you can use the system to give you a list of the payments you must make, and maybe even write the cheques for you!

To operate Sales and Purchase ledgers properly, you need a list of your customers, their names and addresses and other details. You will also need a list of your suppliers on a similar basis.

Note that these customers and suppliers are usually those with whom *credit arrangements* are established. Cash transactions (like petrol, etc) can be dealt with under one convenient nominal account heading.

Nominal Ledger

Properly speaking, the Nominal Ledger records details of a company's Liabilities, Assets and Financial transactions (that is, Income and Expenditure). In other words, it pulls together details of your company's transactions.

Liabilities concern what money the business has had access to or, in other words, what has been made available to it and where it has come from (i.e. creditors and shareholders). You can regard liabilities as how much is owed and to whom.

Assets are what the business has done with the money, or what is surplus to liablilties. A bank's loan to a customer, for instance, is an Asset. To be in good health, a business must have assets at least equal to liabilities, and preferably well in excess of them.

Whereas in a manual system you would expect to regularly transfer (or post) the balances of other ledgers into the Nominal, computer accounting systems do this automatically. They therefore make heavy use of the Nominal Ledger, because it's here that the totals of *all* the areas of income and expenditure your company has are kept. In other words, it summarises or consolidates all the transactions recorded elsewhere.

Reports, such as Balance Sheet and Profit and Loss accounts are then derived from these figures. The *Trial Balance*, for example, is the sum of total credits against debits, available at any time.

In the Nominal Ledger, your company's activities are subdivided under various headings of income and expenditure and given a heading and code number to make it easier to allocate totals to them. For example, there may be a Nominal Account called Hotel Expenses, with a code number of 1400.

The numbering system is best done in consultation with your accountants, because they will probably have to sort out the mess later, but most programs will come with a standard set that you can adapt to your own purposes. Whatever you use, it must be sensible. This is because it's easier to keep track of related headings, and their totals can be combined for easy adding up later. For instance, under the heading of Transport (with a *nominal* code of 2100), you could have petrol (2101), parking (2102), insurance (2103) and so on.

The related numbers can all be added up together and summarised automatically in the balance sheet (numbers must be contiguous for this to happen). Leave plenty of gaps between groups, just in case you need to add more in between later. For example, use 1400 and 1410, so accounts 1401-1409 can be slotted in.

Month end routines

The month-end routine deals with the regulars, like direct debits and rent payments, amongst other things (these are kept in a file which updates the ledgers).

If you don't have direct debits or regular monthly payments, you may not need to bother with this, but doing it is useful anyway because errors can at least be detected early and contained.

Stock control

This keeps track of what items your business has in stock for sale to your customers, and their prices so your invoices can be produced.

A lot of money can be tied up in stock that could be used more efficiently elsewhere. The stock mentioned is that *for sale* — it doesn't necessarily mean anything that you buy as part of the course of your business. For example, if you were a builder, you wouldn't call the bricks used in building a wall *stock* as such, unless you were actually in the business of selling bricks.

Your accountant will need to know stock levels so that the value of your business can be calculated at any time. There will also need to be some sort of depreciation procedure.

Payroll

If used, this will calculate salaries, print payslips, etc.

Job Costing

This will help you keep track of work in progress, especially where work is done over a period of time, for instance in building, where a quote is given for a whole job, rather than just specifying a rate per hour. A job-costing routine will help control costs and issue timesheets which can be used against the payroll module. Parts can be used from stock in a similar way.

Budgeting

A method of presetting targets against which performance can be measured.

Reports

Having all this information is no good if you can't do something with it. Almost all accounts programs have some form of *report procedure* to help you see what's going on. The better programs will allow varying levels of customisation so that you can increase the sophistication of the information you get.

Most of it should be transferable to other programs, such as wordprocessors and the like.

Balance Sheet

This shows the assets of a business and how they are financed at any given time, ordered into three groups; *Assets*, *Liabilities* and *Capital* (or *Equity*).

Audit Trail

The audit trail confirms that every transaction that's been recorded really exists and *vice versa*. It allows you to follow transactions from beginning to end, so you can verify the accuracy of each entry.

This is a most important facility—regardless of any alterations that may have taken place to make your books look neater, the audit trail lists transactions *as they are created*, in strict order. It is not alterable, for obvious reasons.

Setting up

To save time and trouble later, you must set up your system properly from the beginning, because you will naturally not be able to change much subsequently. You will need to know several things before you start, such as who you currently trade with, both selling and buying, and the areas in which your company is active, in terms of expenses, overheads and income. As far as the computer is concerned, you will need to:

- Open personal accounts for each of your customers and/or suppliers (in the *Sales* or *Purchase Ledgers,* respectively) and *Nominal Accounts* to record the results of the transactions between them.

- Next, you need to print them all out, both as security in case the computer blows up and for reference when you need to work with them later (it saves you continually changing to different parts of the program).

- Then enter your opening balances for the date you want to start (from the *1st* of a month).

- Tell the program what VAT rate you're using.

- Tell it how you want your stationery laid out (including balance sheets, etc).

After that, the normal procedure is to let invoices and receipts build up over a period (usually a week), sort them in order, write the account details, including the account reference number and Nominal Code, on the paperwork and place the information inside the computer on a *batch processing* basis, i.e. all in one go. Don't be tempted to lump several invoices as one total. Although this is possible, you may need to unravel the mess later!

At the end of every month, and the year, carry out *month-* and *year-end* routines to consolidate the data and produce reports.

Reports, however, can be produced at any time.

Other tips

Cash received should be treated as a cheque and entered into the bank account, not as Petty Cash.

Sometimes, when you know you're getting a lump sum and you want to pay some bills with it, you can go into the list of *Aged Supplier* accounts, giving the date when the lump sum is due, and get a list of payments falling due before that date.

Try not to use *automatic allocation*, where an amount received is used to cover several outstanding invoices. You can bet the machine won't pick the right ones, so use *manual allocation*.

Keep a separate list of *credit notes*, similar to an order book. Once you've entered credit note details into the system, you must then match them to a corrresponding invoice. If you need to know the *transaction reference* first, you can get this from the audit trail.

Direct debit payments (recurring entries) can be automatically posted monthly, assuming they are for the same amounts. The details are in a file that is run during each month end routine.

Prepayments are for items like rent, which are sometimes paid quarterly in advance. Again, the details are kept on a file that is run during each month-end routine.

To reverse the action of an invoice (you may have made a mistake and only discovered the error after you've posted it), raise a credit note with the same details, post that and redo the original.

Communications

Computers can talk to each other, usually over the telephone lines, but sometimes over dedicated cables joining them up round the office (this is mostly similar to the coaxial stuff used for TV aerials). In fact, much of modern life would grind to a halt if they couldn't; credit card authorisations are done this way and large companies get their sales orders direct from regional offices.

Your company could also have a mainframe computer (the sort that occupies one or two large rooms) containing information you can use in your work. You can connect your computer to it directly and *download* information from it.

It's just the same over the telephone with other peoples' large computers; you can book theatre and airline tickets, or simply connect to a *Bulletin Board* to pass messages to other people with similar interests to yourself. Alternatively, you could use the telephone to keep in touch with the office whilst working from home.

A Bulletin Board, by the way, acts as an electronic noticeboard, where anyone can "pin up" notices for public consumption; some companies use them to handle orders or cope with technical support problems, but there are hundreds of private ones, all free of charge. A bulletin board is just a computer that is permanently switched on and connected to the telephone line, and programmed to answer calls automatically.

Modems

Because the telephone system uses a different way of transmitting electrical signals than computers do, you need a special gadget (called a modem) to change them over.

The computer sends its signals to the modem, which converts them for use on the telephone, and a modem at the other end converts them back again. The reason for using a modem is that it's cheaper than converting the whole telephone system to speak computer language – however, telephone exchanges are becoming digital so, hopefully, modems will eventually not be required.

As with any machinery, some modems do a better job than others, and you need to make sure that those at each end of your communications channel are evenly matched. For example, they must both run at the same speed and use the same rules of communication (called *protocols*).

Protocols are managed by software and control the flow of data over the line, for example, making sure that the sending computer doesn't transmit so fast that the receiving one can't cope.

More powerful software will provide *error checking*, which is intended to make sure that the data that arrives is the same as what was sent.

All you need is . . .

The following items will connect your PC to the telephone system:

- The PC itself, which must have a communications, or serial port based on RS232 standards (RS 422 on a Macintosh). You shouldn't have to worry about the numbers – they're just standards laid down by some committee or other to make sure that computers all send the same signals down the same wires. Your computer should conform to them automatically.

- A modem, which for simplicity should be *Hayes compatible* (that is, follows the standards laid down by the Hayes modem manufactureres in the USA). The modem needs to be connected to the PC's serial port with a cable, but you can get internal modems that plug into a slot inside your computer, so you won't need to bother with a cable.

- Since a computer only does what it's told, you also need *communications software* to send and receive data and save it to disk when necessary. More about software on the next page.

- A telephone line!

How to use your software

Your software must be able to do the following:

- Pretend to be a type of *terminal* that the computer at the other end can recognise. A terminal is used by some large computers to talk to the outside world, and it consists of a screen and keyboard only. There are several types of terminal, none of which behave like an IBM-compatible computer, hence the need for translation. Prestel, for instance, which uses *Viewdata* (as used by travel agents), needs a terminal capable of displaying specialised graphics, so a PC needs to be specially programmed (using terminal emulation) to do so.

- Transfer data to and from each end. Although it's relatively easy to make a connection between two machines over the telephone lines, moving the data concerned is the most important task.

Setting up

Different hardware has different capabilities; just like cars, some computers run faster than others. The equipment at either end of the telephone line must be evenly matched, and your software needs to be set up properly to control it all in terms of:

- **Speed,** or the number of data bits transferred per second. Sometimes, this is referred to as the *baud rate*, although the terms are not strictly interchangeable. Typical baud rates range from 300 to 9600, but the telephone lines are not capable of handling more than 2400 without special error correction procedures (check your software for something called MNP). Actually, quoted speeds higher than 2400 are usually *effective speeds*, where data is compressed as it's sent so more is packed into a smaller space.

- **Parity,** which is a primitive form of error checking, and more or less out of date, so it's usually set to *None* (the other options are *Even* and *Odd*).

- **Data bits**; that is, the number of bits transferred at a time. If you remember, a byte consists of eight bits. If you use Even or Odd parity (above), the eighth bit will be used for error checking, which reduces the chances of transmitting complex characters which need all eight bits to appear on your screen properly.

- **Stop bits**. Because only one cable is used to transmit data, there needs to be some way of telling when each character sent comes to an end, which is what a stop bit is for. It's simply an extra bit that is immediately recognisable as *not* being a character, so the computer knows when the next one starts. If you like, stop bits are there to give the computers a chance to synchronise with each other. Usually set to 1.

- **Handshaking**, or how the flow of data between each *computer* is to be controlled (that is, *hardware only*). There must be a way, for example, for the receiving computer to tell the sending one to stop for a while if it gets a problem. Usually, this will be Xon/Xoff. An alternative is DSR/DTR, or CTS/RTS.

- **Protocol**, which is similar to handshaking, but for use between different *programs* (hardware-based handshaking is a personal matter between the computers). The best general choices are ZMODEM, YMODEM, XMODEM or ASCII, in that order.

All of the above settings can be set from within your communications software, usually at the same time as setting up the telephone number of the computer you want to talk to (look for *Settings....*).

You obviously need to know what settings the receiving computer expects, so you can to talk to it properly; luckily, speed detection on Bulletin Boards is usually automatic, so if you set your program up for 2400 baud, No parity, 8 data bits and 1 stop bit, you shouldn't go far wrong. If you can set handshaking, try Xon/Xoff, or its alternative DSR/DTR, but this should also be automatic.

Also under settings will be the type of terminal your computer is required to pretend to be. VT-100 is a common choice, but TTY, ANSI and PRESTEL are others. You need to set the terminal type so that your keystrokes can be interpreted correctly and the right characters shown on the screen.

Finally, you will need to know which COMmunications port your modem is attached to. A PC usually has two of these, COM1 and COM2, where COM1 is commonly taken up by a mouse, just to make things awkward. If you're not sure, try each one in turn. If your computer freezes up, the COM port you have chosen is already in use by another piece of equipment.

As usual, you can automate things with macros, but communications programs call them *scripts*.

Other modem settings

Aside from speed, your modem may need other instructions in order to make it behave properly.

Typically, this will contain the commands for Tone or Pulse dialling (according to your telephone) or numbers to get you an outside line or other access numbers (for different telephone systems).

A set of standard instructions has evolved from from an original specification by *Hayes*, and American modem manufacturer, which is called the *AT command set*.

For example, if you need to insert a pause in your telephone number (you might be on a telephone exchange which needs a couple of seconds to think to itself), simply use a comma, as with:

```
9,
```

if you need to dial 9 to get an outside line before sending the proper number.

An example of a full dialling command could be:

```
ATDT9,131,36547777789
```

The first letters, **AT**, get the modem's attention, **D** means *Dial*, **T** means *Tone* (you would use **P** for *Pulse*), the **9** gets you an outside line and the commas insert a pause during the process of dialling.

Modem Initialisation String

Sometimes a special set of commands are sent to the modem when the computer starts to wake it up properly. They concern whether the speaker should be on and various other housekeeping settings. Such a string of commands is called a *modem initialisation string*, and is mostly unimportant.

Data Transfer

There are two types of data that can be sent between computers; *Binary* and *ASCII*, and it's important to tell your software what type of data it's dealing with.

ASCII

ASCII we already know about as being the standard way encoding characters in the alphabet, and there's a Carriage Return and Line Feed at the end of each line of an ASCII file. Being straight text, an ASCII file contains no formatting instructions, such as where to start bold or italic printing, where the tabs are, and the like (in other words, there are no hidden codes in the text put there by the software).

The particular thing to note with data files saved in the format of the program that produced them is that "real" Carriage Returns are only found at the end of each *paragraph*.

At the end of each line within any paragraph is a *soft return*, which is put there by the word wrap procedure when it puts the text on the next line automatically. Naturally, different programs have different ways of doing this, so confusion reigns if no particular standards are used, which is where ASCII comes in.

However, it's not safe to assume that conversion to ASCII is done automatically when data is sent, so you must remember to *convert it before you send it.*

Life is never that simple, though.... Although it's easy enough to create an ASCII file from word processed text (just print to disk), it's not so easy the other way round.

To convert from ASCII to native wordprocessing formats, use Search and Replace. You should be able to import the file in ASCII, and the text should be formatted to have a spare line between each paragraph. Use Search and Replace to substitute each Carriage Return (usually signified with ^P, but prepare for surprises) with a symbol (try *), then replace each *pair* of those symbols with one Carriage Return (that's the paragraphs taken care of). Next, replace every single occurrence of the same symbol with a space, and that takes care of the individual lines.

Binary Files

These are files consisting of program code. The problem with these is that, if they are not given special treatment, the odd byte in them may be misinterpreted as an instruction at either end and thoroughly confuse the whole issue.

The classic example is the command sometimes used to denote the end of a text file, which is ^z. This can sometimes appear in a program file in an entirely different context, but will be taken to mean the end of the file, and the one you are transmitting will be cut short in its prime.

9

Under The Hood

The previous chapters have dealt with the basics of what you need to get you started with your computer and its operating system, so you should at least be able to get something out of the most commonly used types of software. This chapter introduces terms that need to be explained before you get on to *Setting Up Your Own System*, in Chapter 10.

The subject matter is technical, but you should find it interesting to read it for its own sake, as it will help you get the very best out of the machinery you are using (although you can drive a car without knowing how the clutch works, you get more out of it if you do).

Hardware Performance

Although computers may have basic similarities (they all look the same on the super-market shelf), performance will differ markedly between them, just the same as it does with cars—it's all too easy to put a big engine in (or a fast processor) and forget to improve the brakes and suspension!

There are two very good reasons why you should make the effort to find out what's inside a typical PC-compatible. The first is to make sure you get one most suited to your needs (should you be getting one yourself—see Chapter 10), and the second is to get the best performance out of what you end up with.

The trick to getting the most out of any machine is to make sure that each component is giving of its best, and then to eliminate potential bottlenecks between them. As you will see in this chapter, different parts of the computer have very different speeds and capabilities which must be matched properly.

You can get a bottleneck simply by having an old piece of equipment that is not designed to work at modern high speeds — since any computer is only as fast as its slowest component, it makes sense to ensure that everything is up to scratch.

Of course, bottlenecks can be due to software as well. A computer is only a machine, after all, and relies on instructions to tell it what to do. If the instructions you issue don't extract the best from it, you will have problems.

This chapter will look at the individual parts of the computer and suggest ways to make them work better, both individually and as a whole.

The Motherboard

This is a large circuit board to which are fixed the *Central Processor*, the *data bus*, *memory* and various other support chips, such as those that control printing, the keyboard, etc. Below is a picture of a typical PC-compatible motherboard (although different computers may put the components in different locations, the basic relationship between them is the same).

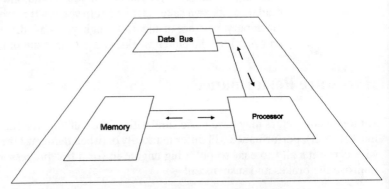

The *Central Processor* does all the thinking, and is told what to do by instructions contained in *memory*, so the two will have a direct two-way connection between them. The *data bus* is actually a part of the Central Processor, although it's treated separately. Extra circuitry in the form of *expansion cards* is placed into *expansion slots* on the data bus, so the basic setup of the computer can be changed easily (for example, you can connect more disk drives or a screen here).

A typical expansion card looks like this:

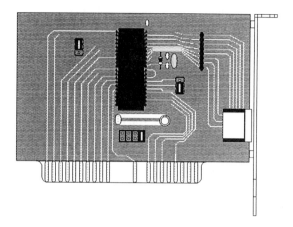

The edge connector along the bottom plugs into a slot on the expansion bus.

Sometimes a *maths co-processor* is fitted to work alongside the main processor. Co-processors are specially built to cope with *floating point* arithmetic (e.g. decimal points). The main processor has to convert decimals and fractions to whole numbers before calculating on them, and then has to convert them back again. If you can make use of a maths coprocessor, you will obviously be better off in terms of speed and efficiency, but it won't be used automatically — your software must be aware of how to use a maths co-processor, otherwise you will not get any benefit (luckily, most are).

Bits and Bytes

Computers talk in *binary language*, which means that they count to a base of 2 (we use 10). When electrical signals are sent around the computer, they are either *On* or *Off*, which matches this perfectly. A state of On or Off is called a **Binary Digit**, or **Bit** for short, and is represented on paper by a 1 for *On* or 0 for *Off* (you can see the same symbols on power switches on electrical appliances).

To place one character on the screen takes eight bits, so when a machine is spoken of as being *eight-* or *sixteen-bit*, it's dealing with one or two letters of the alphabet at the same time — a 32-bit computer can therefore cope with 4 characters in one go.

Because of this, a computer will also count to a base of 16, or in *hexadecimal*, which uses letters as well as numbers, and the order is 0 1 2 3 4 5 6 7 8 9 A B C D E F, as you run out of numbers after 9.

The Central Processor

The chip that was the brains of the original IBM PC was called the 8088, manufactured by Intel. No more need be said about it, except that although it was classified as being 16-bit, it spoke to the data bus with 8 bits (this was to keep the costs down). Thus, when it wanted to send two characters to the screen over the data bus, it had to send them one at a time, rather than both together, so there was an idle state where nothing was done every time data was sent.

> In view of this, you can begin to see that processor speed alone is no guide to performance, and in some cases may even be irrelevant. A slow hard disk, for instance, will always make any processor wait for its data and waste cycles that could be used for serious work.

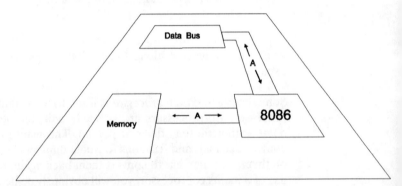

The 80286

The 80286 was introduced in response to competition from other manufacturers. The connections between the various parts of the motherboard became 16-bit throughout, thus increasing efficiency.

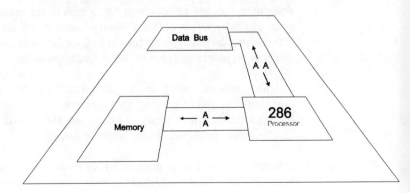

The 80386

The 80386 (DX version, as opposed to the SX – see below) uses 32-bits between itself and memory, but 16-bits towards the data bus, which hasn't really been developed in tandem with the rest of the machine. This is due to the plumbing arrangements – because of its design (based on the technological knowledge of the time), if the data bus is run too fast, you get *electrical noise*, or extra voltages (extra 1s), which will look to the computer like extra data.

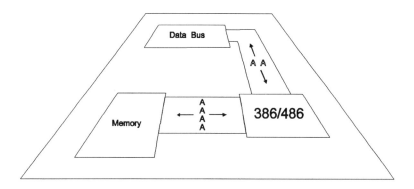

You also now have a speed problem..... The Central Processor may run at 33 Megahertz or so (think of it as miles per hour), but the data bus still runs at 8, because of the original design constraints.

Couple that with memory running at twice the speed of the CPU (so you can use cheap memory chips), not only do you have the equivalent of four-lane motorways narrowing down to dual carriage-ways, you have to slow right down from anything up to 80 mph (or MHz) in the memory area, through 40 at the Central Processor, right down to 8 mph by the time you reach the data bus; more opportunities to waste processing cycles!

The 80386SX

The 80386SX is a 32-bit chip internally, but 16-bit externally to both memory and the data bus. It is a cut-down version of the 80386DX, created both to cut costs and give the impression that the 286 is out of date (which it is). Although it can run 386-specific software, it appears to be a 286 to the machine it is in. At the same clock speed, the 386 SX is around 25% slower than the 386 DX.

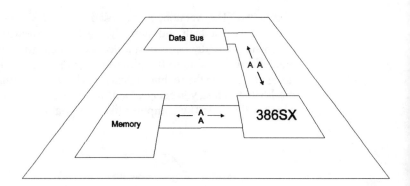

The 80486

To non-technical people (and software), the 80486 is an 80386 (DX) with an on-board maths co-processor and 8K of cache memory. It's not really newer technology as such (although it is second-generation), but better use is made of its facilities. For example, it takes fewer instruction cycles to do the same job, because the design is better.

One advantage is that you can run the motherboard (and the memory) at the same speed as the chip, so there's less overall workload. Another is the speed benefit because the thinking components are all very close together (inside the CPU) and don't have to transfer data over a bus. Generally speaking, at the same clock speed, a 486 will deliver between 2-3 times the performance of a 386, but this won't be so noticeable under most real world situations.

The 80486SX

The 486SX is as above, but with the maths co-processor facility disabled, therefore (generally speaking) you should find no significant difference between it and a 386. Things get more interesting when you want to add a maths co-processor, though. The 387/387SX won't work, and the 487SX either sits alongside or *replaces* the 486SX, depending on your machine, so you're really buying a 486. However, the *Overdrive option* is a better bet, which runs at twice the speed and allows you create a faster computer.

Overdrive/DX2

An Overdrive Chip and a DX2 are more or less the same thing, but the former can be fitted by the end-user (i.e. you), and the latter is intended for manufacturers.

Clock Doubling

The overdrive chip runs at double the speed of the original, which means at twice the speed of the rest of the system. Although this does mean better performance, it will never be the same as having a computer running properly at twice the speed, due to the capabilities of the rest of the motherboard; for example, the bus will still be running at normal speed. However, performance is still good, as code is more often than not executed from the chip's on-board cache, so there's no need to fetch data so often from the system bus.

Summing up

In principle, therefore, the faster the Central Processor is the better, but only if your applications do a lot of thinking and calculation (where the work is centred around the chip) rather than writing to disk. For example, when on a typical wordprocessing task, replacing a 16 Mhz 386 with a 33 MHz one (that's double the speed) will only get you something like a 5-10% increase in practical performance, regardless of what the benchmarks might say. To write your letters faster, you would actually have to reduce the hard disk access time by half.

Bus Types

The expansion bus (where you put your expansion cards) is an extension of the Central Processor, so when adding cards to it, you are extending the capabilities of the CPU itself. It's a route in and out for data between the CPU and any expansion cards on the bus.

The standard data bus is known as the *Industry Standard Architecture* (ISA) bus, and there have been attempts at creating 32-bit versions (e.g. *EISA* or *Micro Channel*), but they haven't exactly taken the world by storm. It happens that the ISA bus is easily able to cope with the data throughput of the devices that may appear on it, but it's a moot point as to whether you would have better equipment with a more capable bus.

The bus itself does no processing – it is merely a pathway for data, but a system called *bus mastering* (available with Micro Channel and EISA) can take the load off the CPU and allow the bus to run independently of it. It's worth noting that, however impressive the capabilities of any bus internally, data still has to get from there to the computer's memory.

ISA

This is the standard 16-bit bus, as supplied in the original AT, and the initials stand for *Industry Standard Architecture*. It runs at 8 MHz, and has a *maximum* data transfer rate of about eight megabits per second on an AT (actually well above the capability of disk drives, or most network and video cards). The *average* data throughput is around a quarter of that.

The majority of expansion boards are made to ISA specifications, and the bus is backwards compatible with the 8-bit cards used on the IBM PC/XT—if the bus is faster than your expansion boards can cope with, you may be restricted to their slower speed.

Its main advantage is that it is a common standard, so many boards are available.

EISA

Stands for *Extended Industry Standard Architecture*. When pushed, EISA is able to transfer data in 32-bit bursts of around 33 mbps (with bus mastering). It is an evolution of ISA and is (theoretically, anyway) backwards compatible with it, including the speed (8 MHz), so the increased data throughput is mainly due to the data bus doubling in size—but you must use EISA expansion cards to get this.

One advantage of EISA (and Micro Channel) is the ease with which you can set up expansion cards—just plug them in and run the computer's configuration software which will automatically detect their settings.

Micro Channel Architecture (MCA)

This is a proprietary standard established by IBM to take over from ISA, and is therefore incompatible with anything else. It comes in two versions, 16- and 32-bit and, in practical terms, is capable of transferring around 20 mbps.

It operates at variable speeds, up to about 14.5 Mhz if it has to, but regular 32-bit transmissions actually run at 10 mbps, and 16-bit at 5 mbps.

Again, there are no switches or jumpers on the cards, so installation is easily done with the Reference software supplied with the computer.

Local Bus

The *local bus* is one more directly suited to the CPU; it's next door (hence local), has the same bandwidth and runs at the same speed, so the bottleneck is less. Data is moved therefore to the local bus at processor speeds.

PCMCIA

A standard originally created for credit-card size memory additions to portable computers. However, versions 2 and 3 cover other peripherals, such as modems and hard disks (they each get thicker in turn). Desk-top computers can also have the slots so that data can be transferred easily. The initials stand for *PC Memory Card International Association*.

Memory

The memory contains the instructions that tell the Central Processor what to do, as well as the data created by the CPU's activities. Since the computer works with bits that are either on or off, memory chips work by keeping electronic switches in one state or the other for however long they are required. Where these states can be changed at will, the memory is known as Random Access Memory, or RAM.

A ROM, on the other hand, is simply a memory chip that has its electronic switches permanently on or off, so they can't be changed, hence the name Read Only Memory.

Memory on the system board is accessed much faster than any on the expansion bus (which generally runs at 8 Mhz). Typically, a 386 or 486 will be able to take up to 32 Mb on board, sometimes with a special 32-bit expansion slot so that the relationship between memory and the CPU is not affected. These are generally non-standard, and you will most likely need one specific to the machine (spares for high-end IBM compatibles are notoriously expensive). Increasing system memory in other ways will always mean large reductions in speed and performance, such as when you place it on a board in the expansion bus, which is 16-bit, of course, and slower.

On systems up to and including the 386, memory runs twice as fast as the processor, which is the reason for the various methods mentioned below of improving performance as an alternative to using fast (and expensive) memory chips. The 486, on the other hand, runs its memory at the same speed as the processor. As it also has an 8K cache, it needs to use the memory bus about 33% less than the 386.

Wait states

Where there are differences between processor and memory speeds, *wait states* help eliminate timing problems. The wait state indicates how many ticks of the system clock the CPU has to wait for everything else to catch up — it will generally be 0 or 1, but can be up to 3. Ways of avoiding wait states include:

- **Page-mode memory**, which is faster than the way memory is used normally, but a more complex logic must be used to control it. The *page address* of data is noted when it's accessed, and if it's the same one as that of the next data needed, *page mode* is invoked to reduce the access time to about half. Otherwise data is retrieved normally from some other page. *Fast page mode* is a quicker version of the same thing, but low capacity chips will have difficulty with it.

- **Interleaved memory,** which divides memory into two or four portions that process data alternately; that is, the CPU sends information to one section while another goes through a refresh cycle (a refresh cycle keeps the electrical charge in the memory chip fresh, which is used to keep the electrical switches on). To put interleaved memory to best use, fill every socket you've got. For example, eight 1 Mb SIMMS are better than two 4 Mb ones.

- A processor **RAM cache,** which is a bridge between the CPU and slower main memory; it consists of anywhere between 32-256K of (fast) Static RAM chips and is designed to predict and retrieve data the CPU is likely to want next. It can make 1 wait state RAM look like that with 0 wait states, without any physical adjustments. On a 486, 64K is usually sufficient, because there's 8K in the chip. The figure is not much different for a 386, either.

Shadow RAM

ROMs are used by parts of the computer that need their own instructions to work properly, such as a video card or cacheing disk controller with a *Translator ROM*. Of course, you could load the instructions from a disk drive, but this is impractical.

ROMs are 8-bit devices, so data access from them will be slow in something like a 386, which uses 32-bit memory. *Shadow RAM* transfers the contents of various ROMs (usually the system and/or video BIOS) directly into *extended memory*, making it run faster, because it now becomes 32-bit (the address of the ROM is changed electronically so the instructions think they are where they should be).

If your applications execute ROM routines often enough, enabling Shadow RAM will make a difference in performance of around 8 or 9%, assuming a program spends about 10% of its time using instructions from ROM. The drawback is that the RAM set aside for this purpose cannot be used for anything else, but the amount is usually minimal.

Random Access Memory

There are several types of Random Access Memory that a program expects to use:

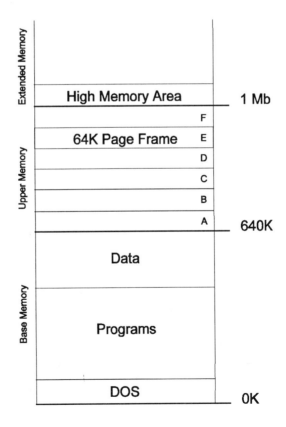

Conventional (or base) memory

This is the first 640K available. It traditionally contains DOS and any programs to be run, plus their data, so the less room the system takes up, the more there is left for the rest.

The original IBM had 20 physical connections between the Central Processor and its memory. Since computers work on the binary system, and therefore count to a base of 2, it's a simple calculation as to how much memory the Central Processor can talk to at once:

$$2^{20} = 1024K$$

DOS was written to run applications inside this bottom 640K block simply because the designers of the original IBM PC decided to.

Upper memory

The next 384K, or the remainder of the 1 Mb that the original PC was designed to work with, was reserved for private use by the computer, so that any expansion cards with their own memory (usually acting as buffers, but ROMs are included as well) could operate safely there without interfering with programs in base memory, or *vice versa*. Typical examples include Network Interface Cards or graphics adapters.

Unused parts of upper memory can be used by DOS to load small programs in, so keeping them away from base memory.

The area is split into regions, A-F, which in turn are split into areas numbered from 0000 to FFFF hexadecimally.

Actually, upper memory starts halfway through Area C. The VGA card will use areas A, B and the first half of Area C (A000-C7FF), and the ROM BIOS will use area F, so the *useable* upper memory area is typically areas D and E. The bit between A000 and C7FF is actually base memory that has been grabbed by the video adapter, and is reclaimable if you don't want to use graphics.

High memory

This is the first 64K (less a few bytes) of extended memory (see below), and is useable only by Intel 286, 386 or 486 based computers that have more than 1Mb of memory installed. It's a quirk in the chip design that can be exploited by DOS to store some of its operating code, leaving yet more available for programs in base memory. It is activated with HIMEM.SYS (MS-DOS) or HIDOS.SYS (DR DOS).

Extended memory

Memory above 1 Mb not otherwise interfered with (see *Expanded memory*, below) is known as *extended memory*, and is not normally useable under DOS, except to provide RAM disks or caches.

Expanded memory

One successful method of breaking the 640K memory limit is a system of physical bank-switching called LIM memory, named after Lotus, Intel and Microsoft, the inventors.

The latest LIM standard (4.0) directly swaps any 16K block of base memory with a similar one of memory above 1 Mb through a 64K block of upper memory called a *window* or *page frame* through which data moves back and forth (see diagram on p 135).

Points to note about LIM are:

- It is only available for data (not program code).

- Programs need to be specially written to use it.

On an 8086 or 286-based machine, expanded memory is usually provided by circuitry on an expansion card, but there are some (not altogether successful) software solutions. 386-based machines have memory management built in to the central processor, so all that's needed is the relevant software to activate LIM (EMM386.EXE or similar).

When manually selecting a page frame, you will need 64K of contiguous upper memory (that is, it needs to be all together!). Various programs will inspect upper memory and tell you how it's being used, and help you place the page frame properly. Try and place it directly next to a ROM, and not in the middle of a clear area, so what's left is as contiguous as possible. A good place is just under the system ROM, at E000.

Buying more RAM

Make sure it has the correct speed. Using faster chips won't speed up the machine directly, but it will allow you to reduce the wait states.

Try and keep the same type of chips in the same banks, which will reduce parity errors. This is particularly important with chips from different manufacturers.

Don't use 16-bit memory boards in a 386 and above.

Hard Disks

Obviously, hard disks do the same job as floppy drives, except that they spin permanently and tend to be non-removable. Floppies are speeded up and allowed to slow down as required.

Inside, hard disks look like this:

Each platter is covered in a magnetic substance and has its own read/write head. All heads move at once when data is requested, giving the best possible speed.

Read/write heads are not in contact with the drive surface, as they are with floppy drives. On a hard disk, they actually float a couple of thousandths of an inch above it, and are also aerodynamically shaped. As the gap between the recording head and the surface is so small (Seagate compare it to a 747 flying at full speed 40 feet above the ground), you can imagine the problems if dust or other contaminants were to get in. This is why hard disks are sealed within a casing filled with inert gas – a good reason for not undoing the screws!

When the power is off on older drives, however, the head may touch the surface, with the obvious dangers when the computer is moved. Unfortunately, similar dangers arise when the computer is switched on, since the flow of power moves the head slightly to the right, scraping the recording medium as it does so.

To protect your data, and prolong hard disk life, it's a good idea to *park* the heads in a neutral area whenever the computer is switched off, so the above problems are not so apparent. This won't stop the head from scraping the surface, but at least it will do so in a safe place!

However, most modern hard disk designs have the head mounted on a solenoid which is designed to spring upwards when power is turned off. Still newer ones have the heads in contact with the disk, to get closer tolerances, but supported by fluid, so parking the heads is not so important, and may even confuse the issue.

Performance considerations

Hard disk activity is the main performance consideration in any system, and a slower machine with a fast hard disk will outperform a fast one with something less efficient, since even the slowest processors (and data buses) spend around half their time waiting for disks to catch up. The hard disk is controlled by specialised circuitry, and this should also be considered — differences between components in the drive chain can account for variations in performance as high as 20%.

A typical hard disk transfers data at a rate of rather less than 1 Megabyte per second (300-400K in fact), and even those at the top of the range only stretch to 2! This is a lot less than even the ISA bus can handle, so *data throughput* is as important as the *access time* when comparing drives (see below).

Hard disk performance is actually measured in many ways, including:

Average access time	The time it takes to locate data at a specific location on the drive.
Track to track access time	The time it takes to move from one track to the next.
Sector access time	How many sectors can be retrieved in one second.
Transfer rate	How much data can be transferred to the controller in a particular time.
Seek time	The time taken for the drive to locate a particular sector.

Each of the above is only one aspect, though. They should all be considered in combination, together with the hard disk controller's capabilities, but don't concentrate on the wrong one. Databases use disks a lot, but for *searching*, not transferring data, so access time is important. On the other hand, graphic files are typically large (an A4 page takes up 1 Mb of space) so the data transfer rate will be important.

Actually, the best way to speed up a drive is..... Don't use it!! See if you can use a RAM disk for many of the operations that could be performed by a hard disk; e.g. for temporary files.

Hard disk controllers

A 1:1 interleave disk controller (see *Glossary*) is able to read an entire track of the disk in one revolution, and should be the minimum standard to aim for, in conjunction with a hard disk with less than about 20 *ms* access time and a data transfer rate of above 512K per second.

Sometimes, in an attempt to boost data transfer rates, more powerful controllers will employ *read ahead buffering* to bring in more data than is actually requested, so the next disk access takes place from the buffer memory, and thus is faster (assuming the next sector is what's needed). Luckily, the repetitive nature of computing tasks means that much of the data circulating round a machine is needed again and again, so this works quite well.

The next step up from this is *cacheing*, which loads frequently used data into more substantial amounts of cache memory, rather than mere buffers. Caches are designed to help bridge the gap between different parts of the computer that operate at different speeds — the difference is that cacheing will try to anticipate your disk needs, whereas buffers read blindly and just act as holding zones for data.

Up to a point, the larger the cache and the more efficient the cacheing procedures are, the better the *hit rate* you will get (a hit occurs when the requested data is found in the cache). However, note that cacheing only helps on *subsequent* disk access. The first time round, your data will be freshly read at the internal transfer rate.

Also, if your cache is too large, you may find that more time is spent managing it than retrieving data.

If your operating system does its own cacheing, you may just confuse the issue and get slower performance as a result. The worst use of a cache is infrequent, large and non-recurring disk writes; once the cache is flushed, you are left with redundant data and will have to start all over again, at the normal transfer rate direct from disk.

Try and place print queues (e.g with Print Manager in Windows) in memory, otherwise data will be saved to disk, read again, written yet again to a print queue and copied to an output port.

Cacheing controllers

Cacheing disk controllers use large amounts of on-board memory (say, 1-16 Mb) to reduce disk access time down to 1 or so milliseconds in a typical situation. Data throughput will also be increased markedly.

When data from disk is requested, the controller loads up with as much of the hard disk's contents as its memory can cope with, and takes what it needs from there. The end result is similar to having your hard disk data in a RAM disk.

As it isn't multi-tasking, DOS has to wait for a process to finish before it can get on with something else, so you can't get back to writing your letter whilst data is being saved to disk. A cacheing controller, on the other hand, will be able to accept the data, let the PC get on with whatever else it wants to and write the data to disk in its own time. If your operating system can do this already (say, in normal system memory), you're just duplicating things; if the data is in the operating system's cache, the controller won't be asked anyway, so you'll be wasting money.

If your typical application is CPU intensive (lots of number crunching), then you may not necessarily get much out of disk cacheing, except maybe when moving large files around. Databases will benefit, on the other hand, because they are continually writing and reading temporary files to and from disk.

It can be better to use system memory as a disk cache, because this will be 32-bit. On a controller in the ISA bus it will be 16-bit and still provide a bottleneck.

Common Interfaces

The interface is the connection between the hard disk and the expansion bus. Note that ESDI and SCSI drives require special hard disk controllers; as the controlling circuitry is on the drive itself, they will not work with ST-506 drives. IDE drives use an adapter in the bus.

ST-506

A standard established by Seagate in 1980, typically using the MFM data encoding method (see below) to transfer data serially at a rate of less than 1 Mb per second. ST-506 is out of date.

ESDI

The *Enhanced Small Device Interface* offers up to four times the throughput of ST-506, of which it is a direct descendant. It also transmits in serial, but interpretation of various information bits is left to the drive rather than the controller, hence the transfer rate of up to 2.5 Mb per second (a higher density of sectors per track helps).

Data transfer rates actually depend on the components in the drive chain; controllers must be matched to drives, meaning that a controller cannot handle faster drives than itself, although slower ones will be OK. In other words, a 10 MHz controller must match a 10 MHz drive (or less).

The ESDI standard offers higher capacity drives than IDE (1 GB or more), and a more stable platform than SCSI, both mentioned below. Access times tend to be fast, and ESDI controllers are best used with an EISA bus for maximum performance.

IDE (embedded AT)

The term IDE, or *Integrated Drive Electronics* is popularly used to describe an intelligent drive that communicates directly with the AT expansion bus through a connection on the computer motherboard although, strictly speaking, the term includes SCSI, discussed below.

A small host board allows the drive to communicate with the computer, transmitting only data, not drive control information.

In theory, data transfer speeds can be up to three times higher than ESDI (IDE transmits in parallel), up to 4 Mb per second, but this depends on several factors, such as bus clock speeds and other hardware in the computer. Mainly, the problem is that many IDE drives are actually reworked older types, instead of being designed from new, so the rate of data extraction from the disk in the end is sometimes similar to ESDI.

IDE drives are easy to install, and low in cost relative to performance, but few are larger than 350 Mb in size. Cacheing *controllers* are not generally available for IDE drives, although some cacheing host adapters are.

SCSI

The *Small Computer Systems Interface* is an IDE-based *system* (rather than an interface as such, due to the many interpretations) that also transmits data in parallel, as well as having the highest data transfer rate (up to 5 Mb per second for SCSI-1). As the drive is intelligent, a drive's vital statistics can be hidden from applications — for example, the storage space provided will appear as sequentially numbered blocks rather than cylinders and heads.

Data transfer speeds can be impressive (5 Mb/sec – 10 with SCSI 2), and large capacity drives are common. They can also be daisy-chained together, allowing for greater flexibility when expanding (in theory, a SCSI bus can cater for eight devices, but many features are optional, so watch out for compatibility). Each device can be a *target* or an *initiator* with reference to a request. Because the drives are intelligent, an initiator can hand over a task and not necessarily wait for its completion, so getting on with something else. Reconnection can be made later on to tidy things up, which is good for multi-user or network systems.

SCSI 2 is a more compatible version of the original standard, which has features that enhance speed, called *Fast SCSI* and *Wide SCSI*. These increase the clock rate or the date path, respectively. SCSI 3 expands this even further.

Data Encoding Methods

This is the way the data is actually recorded to the disk.

MFM

Uses 17 sectors per track, typically found on ST-506 drives.

RLL

This uses 26 sectors per track, but requires higher quality media than MFM. Although an RLL controller will format an MFM drive, it's not the case the other way round. Most modern drives use RLL, including IDE, ESDI and SCSI.

Screen displays

Serious computer use demands a monitor, whether colour or monochrome (black and white is monochrome). A monitor is essentially a (high quality) TV with the tuning section stripped out so that the generated picture signal goes more or less straight to the screen without picking up anything nasty on the way. This signal can be sent separately down several wires at once, such as Red, Green and Blue (RGB) together with the signals needed to synchronise the lot, or all together down two wires (including sound), which is known as a *composite signal*, for obvious reasons. Composite signals give a lower quality than straight RGB, again because of the greater chance of introducing unwanted effects.

Not all software will be able to run successfully on all screens, even though the resolution may be correct. For example, graphic art programs actually instruct the screen to run at different speeds, which is naturally impossible if the screen is not capable of switching to them.

Unless it has an auto-detect capability, your software will have to be *installed* to take account of the screen you have.

Smaller Macs have very small (9") screens, but the resolution is high enough for this not to matter. Later versions come with colour.

On an IBM-compatible, you will find the following types of screen:

Monochrome Display Adapter (MDA)

This is the screen display fitted to the original IBM PC. Its resolution is very high and the screen characters are therefore very detailed and easily readable. However, only text characters can be displayed, which may be green, amber or red on a black background.

Hercules Graphics Adapter

As the Monochrome Display Adapter could only display text, programs that wanted to show pictures (e.g. graphs) were unable to use it. A company called Hercules designed a display adapter that could show graphics, which rapidly became a standard in its own right.

Colour Graphics Adapter

Commonly known as CGA, this was IBM's attempt to cater for the growing computer games market of the time. As a result, it was good for crude pictures, but very little else. As the resolution is low, text shown on this screen tends to be made up of large dots and usually has to be made more readable with odd colour combinations. In addition, the screen display was not programmed properly and tends to suffer from excessive flicker when the picture changes, which is very annoying. CGA is very much out of date and if you've got it already (on a *very* old computer!), you're stuck with it, but don't even think of getting it otherwise.

EGA

If you have an older computer, you may have the *Enhanced Graphics Adapter*, which displays 640 pixels by 350. It's perfectly adequate for most purposes, where your programs only require to display text, but loses out when you need advanced graphics. Its cost is so near to that of VGA that it's not worth considering, unless you've got it already. EGA has been superseded by VGA (see below).

VGA

The *Video Graphics Array* is the highest resolution standard-issue graphics display you can buy for the IBM and compatibles, and any reference to *Super VGA* indicates the resolution and amount of colours that can be shown on the screen at the same time. For standard VGA, this is 16, but this can be increased to 256 by raising the amount of memory on the video circuit board responsible for driving the screen.

On any screen, the picture is made up of tiny dots, called *pixels*. Standard VGA has 640 pixels across the screen, and 480 down, with 16 colours being displayed at the same time. Super VGA screens are capable of displaying 800 pixels across and 600 down, for which the screen has to be driven at a faster speed, because it has to show more information in the same space of time. It is actually possible to speed up a screen to get 1024 x 768, but you need more expensive equipment for this.

Most people are happy with 16 colours, and the less you want to show at the same time, the better the display performance will be, as there will be less screen redrawing.

VGA is also available in mono (black and white) although, in practice, the "mono" will be various levels of grey.

Graphics accelerators (S3-based)

There are differences between VGA cards as well. Some are very much faster than the average, but the cost will reflect this. *Graphic accelerator cards* are becoming very common, that have the ability to take the load off the Central Processor and handle the screen display themselves.

Setting up your own system

Sooner or later, you will want to run your own system, either for home or business, and this chapter will help you make the right choices.

Software

It may seem strange to deal with this first, but it's actually most important:

> **You find the software, *then* find the computer that runs it!**

Luckily, you're pretty sure of doing it successfully the other way round, because there are thousands of programs already written, and mostly useable, for the types of computer found in business (IBM or Mac), so you're fairly safe if you have your computer already. However, if you're getting into the realms of equipping large companies, where the basic hardware is a bit off the beaten track and can cost upwards of £20,000, you would be well advised to follow the above rule.

Another thing to note about software is that there is no Sale Or Return, so you will have to buy whatever you think will do the job (if you can believe the brochures) and live with it forever, unless you've got the money to try various things. Luckily, you can get demo disks of most software. These will either be an animated slide show that you can't interfere with, and therefore will get very little benefit from, or cut-down versions of the real program, which are infinitely more useful.

There are some good, cheap programs around, but you have to kiss a lot of frogs to find a Prince.... *Shareware* is a common practice, where an author will write a program and make it available on a trial basis. If you end up using it, you are expected to send in a modest fee to get the manuals and the full version.

Be careful, though! You can spread Shareware around, provided you copy *all* the files and don't make a profit, but it is ILLEGAL to make copies of *any* software (aside from security copies, and even that is suspect), let alone give it to your friends to try out.

Latest Editions

Contrary to what the manufacturers tell you, there's usually no need to get the latest edition of any software, unless it's actually had problems fixed (in which case it shouldn't have been on sale in the first place and you shouldn't have to pay for the upgrade), or has a facility that you desperately need.

Many programs which did an excellent job at the start have been subject to "upgrade fever", where the manufacturers put in so many additional features they think will be attractive to buyers that they lose sight of their original direction, and the software actually becomes less useable.

Hardware

The computer is only the beginning of the story. You certainly need a printer to present your work in a meaningful way, and possibly a modem to transmit data over the telephone lines. All this extra equipment adds to your costs, including the little things, such as a connection lead for said printer (which will have a markup of about 200%). A lot of supposed bargains advertised in the magazines don't include the odds and ends, the purchase of which boosts your cash outlay to near enough the recommended retail price anyway. So there's another rule – the cheapest is not necessarily the best.

A little common sense is involved in buying; if the only software you use runs the screen in black and white, there's little point in buying a colour one. Neither is there any point in buying an expensive laser printer if your software isn't written to drive anything more powerful than a dot matrix.

The cheaper the system you buy, the steeper the learning curve required to operate it properly. In this case, you will almost definitely need somebody at the end of a phone to answer questions as they arise, and you won't necessarily get this from a High Street store, who may only be interested in shifting as many boxes as possible.

The keyword is *cost-effectiveness*, or the most efficient use of your money. Pick a level of expenditure and try to stick to it, because there will always be the temptation to spend just that little bit more to get a better machine. The best way to gauge this is the percentage of extra money spent for the percentage better performance you will get. For example, spending another 5% to get a full 386 rather than a 386 SX is worth doing, but it may not necessarily be such a good deal to spend another 25% to jump to a 486, unles you specifically want particular features that only a 486 can provide.

If you buy a clone, you can always keep the disk drives, case, etc and just change the motherboard later, as they all tend to be a standard size (however, this is not so easily done with an XT).

DOS-based programs are relatively undemanding in terms of memory. If you plan to run Windows, however, you need a 386SX with *at least* 4 Mb RAM (preferably 8) and a largish hard disk (around 80 Mb plus). Ignore what it says on the boxes!

Secondhand

If you're buying secondhand, you'll find that the onus is on you to get what you want, because the law says "Buyer Beware!". There's no legal obligation for the seller to tell you anything, though there is a moral obligation to tell the truth when asked a specific question. Your problem, therefore, is to ask the correct questions!

There's not an awful lot to go wrong on secondhand equipment, since only the disk drives are moving parts as such. Test those for reading and writing by copying files back and forth, and scrounge a coffee from the seller so that you can keep the computer running (on his electricity) for as long as possible to check if any heat-related snags turn up—there may be one or two items inside that get abnormally hot and cause the thing to hang after a while. Beware of buying untested single components, if you ever get far enough down the road to start taking the things to bits.

As far as price goes, anything is worth what somebody will pay for it. Most people ask for more than they expect, but some ask for what they want. It's a bit like buying a car in that if you want it for a specific purpose and the price is cheap enough, it doesn't matter that the registration is old and the depreciation is quite heavy and that you may not be able to get an awful lot for it if you come to sell it. Be warned—some computers depreciate rapidly, like some cars; it doesn't matter how old they are, they're still only worth £20!

Many computer magazines carry small ads, and you will get a good idea of prices from those. A rule of thumb is to take the proper retail price (assuming it's a current model), half it and add or subtract a small amount according to condition.

Auctions

There is only one reason why equipment is in an auction – it can't be sold anywhere else. Granted, there are occasions when genuine liquidation items get into one but, generally speaking, auction items are unsaleable otherwise. You've only got to think about a car auction to see the point.

As a result, nothing on offer is worth even half the full retail price. For one thing, it might not work and, for another, it might cost you more to get it going than if you'd bought something decent in the first place.

Also, the machine you want is almost always the last to be called, so you've got to wait all day for it to come up and, if it's that desirable, other people will be after it, as well!

Types of PC-compatible and their uses

IBM-compatible computers are referred to by the chip inside for shorthand, hence "286" or "386".

XT

Although out of date, XT class machines based on the Intel 8086 or 8088 chip (or equivalent) are still useful for basic wordprocessing, spreadsheets and databases where speed isn't particularly required; however, later software may not run. You can place high quality peripherals, like colour screens, on if you want, but it really isn't worth it.

Unless you know absolutely and positively that you will never require anything more powerful, don't bother buying one unless it's very, very, cheap.

286

Good for almost anything, although earlier designs are no faster than XTs. Memory management is not as sophisticated as with a 386 or above, especially when it comes to Expanded Memory. The differential between a 286 and a 386SX is so small that it's not cost-effective to get one of these new unless it's ridiculously cheap.

386SX

A cut-down 386, but useful only as an entry-level system, because the differential between it and a 386DX is too small to worry about. It should come with a Super VGA screen and at least a 40 Mb hard disk and 2 Mb of RAM (4 Mb if you want to run Windows). Runs any software.

386

The most cost-effective machine to aim for when buying new, although it is officially out of date. Get the fastest possible, which should be 40 MHz.

486

Bear in mind that, for all practical purposes, a 486 is a 386 with a maths co-processor built in. Although it is faster than a 386, the extra cost is disproportionate to the performance gained.

Taking your computer away

Before you take your computer away, and to save you coming all the way back into town (because naturally you live miles away from the shop and you can't park next to it and it's late on Saturday afternoon and you work all week and will have to wait till at least next Saturday to get anything you've forgotten) please note the following absolute minimum list of equipment you will need to get you up and running.

- Computer with all items listed in the manual, including keyboard.

- Monitor or screen—with connecting lead and correct plugs at each end. Can your PC drive your particular monitor?

- Spare disks—enough to make copies of your program disks and to practice on.

- Disk drives—usually these are integrated, but you may be buying a portable with an external disk drive.

- You will need a Utilities and/or System disk (in addition to the programs you propose to use), which will contains the housekeeping facilities you will need to start everything off.

- Printer with lead (and correct plugs!), tractor/cut sheet feeder and the right sort of paper to match the feeder.

- This book and, if you feel brave, the relevant manuals for your machine.

- Sufficient plugs to plug everything in with. You will probably also need a 4-socket extension lead to keep everything tidy.

- Mouse/Joystick.

Unless you've got something totally non-standard, the above list should cover things until you get addicted to going to the computer shop and drinking their coffee.

Without being rude, check that all of the above works before you accept anything. If your dealer can't be bothered, then he's obviously a box-shifter so take your custom somewhere else. It's well worth taking a little trouble in the long run to get a dealer who will provide some sort of after-sales service, even if he is a little more expensive or a little farther away than you wanted.

Setting up your computer

Now you've got it home....... how do you put it all together?

Plugs and sockets

Sockets generally will only accept a certain type of plug a certain way round, so you don't need to force anything. If you do, there's something wrong!

The back of your computer will look something like this:

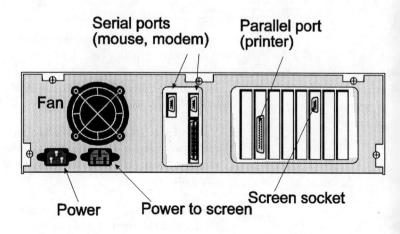

Usually, the monitor has two leads, one for the mains power and one for the display signals, which will each fit into a socket in the base unit. The plug on the end of the signal lead will look like this:

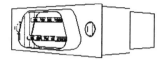

Some monitors are different, of course; *a VGA monitor lead has 15 pins*.

The computer's base unit will also have a mains lead, and the keyboard will plug in somewhere as well. This is usually a 5-pin DIN plug (as found on audio systems) or a smaller one found on IBM PS/2s. It may have a small keyboard symbol on the case to identify it.

A mouse will either plug into a serial port, or a hole similar to a PS/2 keyboard socket. Again, there may be a mouse symbol to identify it.

A serial plug on a mouse will look like the one below; it's like a monitor plug, but has holes instead of pins. You may also find a 25-pin version on older computers.

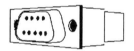

A printer's connection lead will have a plug similar to a monitor's signal plug, but will be wider (with 25 pins). The connector at the other end will look like this:

Tuning for performance

The remainder of this chapter builds on the knowledge gained in *Under The Hood* and examines how to use DOS to get the best performance from your computer. Further information should be sought in the DOS manuals.

System Configuration Files

DOS looks for two files in the root directory when it starts; the settings and commands in them are used to set your computer up the way you want it. The correct setting up of both the CONFIG.SYS and AUTOEXEC.BAT files is the key to getting the best out of your PC. They are created and edited with a text editor that creates ASCII files (see Appendix C).

Symbols used in command descriptions

[ ]   Square brackets indicate optional use of the data between them (don't type the brackets).

| A choice between options (e.g. ON|OFF is equal to On *or* Off). Just make one choice, and don't type the bar itself. On most keyboards, the | symbol is shown with a gap in the middle and is usually obtained by SHIFTing the backslash (\) key.

d: A disk drive, e.g. C:

n   A number you type in.

CONFIG.SYS

This file contains instructions that extend the capabilities of DOS, either by adjusting how certain resources are used (e.g. memory), or loading specialised software for devices that DOS is not geared up to cope with, such as plotters or tape streamers.

The software loaded from CONFIG.SYS actually becomes *part of DOS*, unlike commands run from AUTOEXEC.BAT, which *run under* DOS.

The file must be in the root directory of the boot disk and, in theory, the commands can be entered in any order; however, some commands must be issued first so that others based on them can work.

Within these constraints, to help make best use of upper memory, experiment with the loading order, because program sizes can be deceptive. For example, you may have many programs that won't load in to upper memory even though there's plenty available. This is because they may take more memory to get themselves set up than is needed for their normal size; the mouse program typically uses 60K before shrinking down to about 15.

The definitive CONFIG.SYS file (for DOS 5.0, anyway) could look like that below. It is fully taken to pieces and explained shortly (for DR DOS, see later):

```
DOS=HIGH,UMB
DEVICE=C:\DOS\HIMEM.SYS
DEVICE=C:\DOS\EMM386.EXE RAM|NOEMS [2048]
DEVICEHIGH=C:\DOS\RAMDRIVE.SYS 1024 /E
FILES=30
BUFFERS=2
LASTDRIVE=D
SHELL=C:\COMMAND.COM C:\ /P /E:192 /F
COUNTRY=044,,C:\DOS\COUNTRY.SYS
STACKS=0,0
FCBS=1,1
```

Note that the list above is meant to cover many possibilities, and you can't use commands that aren't relevant to your machine, or which aren't supplied with your version of DOS (check the manual); for example, EMM386.EXE is only useable in 386-type machines and above, and is supplied with DOS 5. If you have a 286, leave EMM386.EXE out (if you don't have DOS 5, you haven't got it anyway). Also, make any adjustments for paths, memory, and other variations relevant to your machine (it was written for a 486 with 8 Mb of RAM).

Line 1	Tells DOS to load itself up into the *High Memory Area* and to use any *Upper Memory Blocks* it may find, increasing the amount of *base memory* for programs and data.
Line 2	Activates the *High Memory Area* so that DOS can actually load into it.
Line 3	Loads an *Expanded Memory Manager* for 386-type computers and above (leave it out for 286s).

You have the choice of creating a page frame or not, by specifying *RAM* or *NOEMS*. With NOEMS, of course, you get another 64K of Upper Memory to play with, because the page frame won't be created.

You can also specify the amount of memory to be allocated as Expanded. The default is 256K; here it is 2 Mb.

Line 4   This line loads the software that creates a RAM disk or, in other words, sets aside a portion of memory to behave as if it were a disk drive, so you can get some speed. The default is 64K, which is usually next to useless, so 1 Mb is specified here.

DEVICEHIGH instructs DOS to load RAMDRIVE.SYS high; that is, into upper memory.

The /E switch tells DOS to use *extended memory* in which to create the RAM disk. You can use *base memory* or *expanded* if you wish, but using the former reduces memory available for programs and the latter is less efficient.

Line 5   Here you specify the amount of files that can be open at any one time. DOS automatically allows eight, to cover printers, serial ports, etc, that it expects to find on a PC, but you will find 30 to be more sensible. Some programs require more, but these are rare. Each file mentioned here takes 59 bytes of base memory away from your programs.

Line 6   Buffers are small amounts of memory used as temporary holding areas for data *en route* to a part of the computer that may be busy and cannot accept it.

Each buffer is 512 bytes in size, which coincides with the size of a sector on a hard disk. You can have up to 99 buffers, but the more you allocate, the more memory you use. Up to 48 can be placed in the High Memory Area if DOS is loaded there, but you won't get much performance benefit above 50 anyway.

The amount of buffers specified here doesn't matter if it's less than 48 and destined for the High Memory Area, but if you're using disk cacheing, reduce it to 10 or below anyway, otherwise you might confuse the computer.

You will probably have to experiment with this figure to find the best one for your circumstances.

Line 7   The last drive letter allocated in your system. If you have RAM disks, CD-ROMs, or other devices that use a drive letter, you need to tell DOS about them here because it assumes you only have 5 drives; that is, up to E.

Unfortunately, each entry takes up 88 bytes of memory, so it makes sense to specify less drives if you have less, so you save memory.

Note that the next *network* drive letter starts *after* this one.

Line 8   SHELL is an environment variable that indicates where COMMAND.COM is, which is the program that decides what to do with your commands (as well as containing the internal ones).

When it loads, it splits itself in half, and loads into each end of base memory; that is, just above DOS and just below the 640K barrier.

The top half is often kicked out of memory by programs that are tight for space, so DOS needs to be able to find it again for reloading. The second part of the command tells COMMAND.COM itself where to find its other half.

The *environment space* is an area where DOS keeps details about its environment. The /E switch used here allocates the specific amount of 192 bytes because the default is 512 bytes, which is usually way over what people usually need (unless you have long PATH commands — see AUTO-EXEC.BAT, below).

The /P switch both disables the first COMMAND.COM's ability to unload itself (you can load more than one when chaining), and also makes it search for AUTO-EXEC.BAT.

/F makes a process abort immediately if there is an error accessing a disk; it saves you a keystroke later on.

Line 9

The country you're in needs to be specified because computers assume they're in the USA unless told otherwise, and you will get the wrong date and time settings.

The numbers are loosely based on the telephone system, and the space between the commas is for the *code page number*, should you change that as well.

COUNTRY.SYS is the file where DOS keeps details about the countries concerned, and its location is specified here.

Line 10

Stacks are small amounts of memory used to store details of what the computer was doing when an *interrupt* occurs (such as a mouse movement). When the interruption ceases, the computer takes the details out of stacks again and resumes from where it left off.

The default is 9 stacks of 128 bytes each (or *9,128*), but if you specify *0,0* as shown here, no memory is allocated at all. Most programs do their own stack handling anyway, so stacks aren't usually needed, but Windows is lazy and gets DOS to do its work, so it needs *9,256*.

Line 11   *File Control Blocks* are an older method of dealing with open files (as opposed to using FILES =). The default is 4, so you save 176 bytes by specifying 1 here.

DR DOS

Here's the same CONFIG.SYS for DR DOS:

```
HIDOS=ON
DEVICE=C:\DRDOS\EMM386|HIDOS.SYS /B=FFFF
/F=AUTO
HIDEVICE=C:\DRDOS\VDISK.SYS 1024 /E
FILES=30
BUFFERS=2
LASTDRIVE=D
SHELL=C:\COMMAND.COM C:\ /P /E:192
COUNTRY=044,,C:\DOS\COUNTRY.SYS
STACKS=0,0
FCBS=1,1
```

You will notice that the commands are more or less similar, but the differences are detailed below.

Line 1   DR DOS's version of DOS = HIGH. Upper Memory Blocks are opened automatically.

Line 2   DR DOS's way of activating the HMA, like HIMEM.SYS. Use as appropriate to your machine, with the command switches to vary their operation. /B = FFFF forces DR DOS into the HMA. /F = AUTO means find a space for the page frame automatically, assuming you use EMM386.SYS (use /F = NONE if you don't want one).

Line 3   The same as DEVICEHIGH in MS-DOS.

AUTOEXEC.BAT

This is a batch file that lives in the root directory of the system disk (usually C:). It is run immediately after COMMAND.COM has been loaded (after CONFIG.SYS), and typically contains DOS commands that are run once only; usually at the start of a working session with your computer. All batch commands are valid, and it may look like this:

```
@ECHO OFF
LOADHIGH C:\DOS\FASTOPEN.EXE C: 256
LOADHIGH C:\DOS\KEYB.COM UK
LOADHIGH C:\DOS\DOSKEY.COM /bufsize=192
PATH C:\DOS;\UTILS;\BAT;\WINDOWS
PROMPT $p$g
SET TEMP=C:\TEMP
```

Note the memory-resident commands (TSRs) that have been loaded *before* the PATH or SET commands, or other variables. This is because each program gets a copy of the environment space as it loads, and if you have a lot in the environment (like long PATH commands), you use memory more than once for the same information. Otherwise, each line means:

Line 1   Don't display this line, and don't display the following commands as they are executed.

Line 2   FASTOPEN is a program that loads the disk index into memory so it's quicker to find files. The drive it operates on is also specifed, and the size of the memory to be set aside for the purpose. LOADHIGH is a DOS 5 instruction to load FASTOPEN into the Upper Memory Area. FASTOPEN probably doesn't make much difference if you have disk cacheing, and it's only really useful if your programs access disks a lot, such as databases.

Line 3   Specifies the keyboard driver to be used.

Line 4   Loads a *command line editor*; aside from allowing you to edit mistakes as they happen, DOSKEY is useful for recycling your past commands so you don't have to type them again.

Line 5	Establishes a search path for programs. Each entry is separated by a semi-colon.
Line 6	Sets up the prompt to display the current directory.
Line 7	Sets up a *variable* that can be interrogated by programs to find out specific information about the computer. In this case, it's where to place temporary files. You can add your own if you wish (see the SET command).

You can add any other commands you may wish to be run automatically as your computer starts up. For example, you might want your wordprocessor ready for action straight away. Be wary of including batch files in AUTOEXEC.BAT, though; either place the name of the batch file you wish to chain to at the end of AUTOEXEC.BAT or use the CALL command to run it and go back to the original file.

DR DOS

The DR DOS version is similar, but with the following exceptions:

```
@ECHO OFF
HILOAD C:\DRDOS\FASTOPEN 256
HILOAD C:\DRDOS\KEYB UK+
PATH C:\DOS;\UTILS;\BAT;\WIN-
DOWS;\OSUTILS;\WS5
PROMPT $p$g
SET TEMP=D:\TEMP
```

Line 2	HILOAD is used instead of LOADHIGH.
Line 3	The + sign is used to indicate an enhanced keyboard.

Command-line editing is built in, so a program like DOSKEY is not required. In DR DOS, this facility is turned on and off with in the CONFIG.SYS file, using the HISTORY command.

Productivity

The remainder of this chapter provides a few productivity tips to help you get the most out of DOS.

Batch files

Comments

Unfortunately, using REM (or ;) slows batch file execution down, because each line is read in turn. A better way is to have GOTO instruction before your comments (say, GOTO ENDREM), and a *label* called ENDREM after them, so the comments are skipped over and ignored, e.g.:

```
GOTO ENDREM
Suitable comments
:ENDREM
```

Variables

Variables are dummy arguments that allow you to create a batch file in principle and add the details when you run it, by using symbolic names instead of real ones. This is really helpful if you would otherwise have to create lots of batch files to cover all the clients you have, for example. By using variables, you can make one do for all of them. Alternatively, you may choose to create a batch file that copies *any* file whose name is provided on the command line.

The symbol %0 is reserved for the name of the batch file itself, but there are nine others for whatever you want.

Every time DOS sees %1, it substitutes the text you included in the command when the batch file started. %1 stands for the first text, %2 for the second, and so on, up to 9.

```
@echo off
copy %1 a:
del %1
```

The above is a batch file called MOVE.BAT. The filename represented by the variables (%1 in this case) must be included in the command line, e.g.

```
MOVE BANK.LTR
```

Environment variables are permanently established strings of information in the environment space that can be used by programs, but can also be used in batch files (see also SET). Very useful for storing user names and having programs configure themselves according to who is using the computer.

Debugging batch files

Make liberal use of ECHO (so you can see the commands as they are executed) and PAUSE (to stop the file at opportune moments).

Switch BREAK = ON and OFF as appropriate within your file so you get more chance of stopping it if things go wrong (the BREAK command allows you to stop a running process).

Appendix A

Everyday DOS Commands

Everyday Commands used

Everyday DOS Commands mentioned in Chapter 3 are listed here in alphabetical order here, including those used in CONFIG.SYS, AUTOEXEC.BAT and other batch files. Please note that not all information is given; only that which is needed for daily use. As they are meant to cover many situations, the following details should not be regarded as authoritative (although the information given is accurate), as the intention of this book is to be a handy reference guide and not a rehash of the manuals — refer to them for full details.

Used in batch files to suppress the display of the line it is on.

Format:

```
@command
```

Comments:

Most often used at the start of the traditional first line of every batch file, which is:

```
@ECHO OFF
```

This is not valid in earlier DOS versions, so try:

```
@ECHO OFF
ECHO OFF
```

to cater for all possibilities.

BUFFERS

Buffers are small blocks of memory that hold information being read from or written to disk.

Format:

```
BUFFERS=nn
```

Comments:

nn is a number from 3-99, but the default is 15. The more buffers created, the less memory there is for programs and data, which could result in things actually running slower! Between 10 and 30 is sensible, but a large hard disk, you may need more. Up to 40 Mb, use 20 buffers, and increase by 10 for every 40 Mb thereafter, up to 50.

Sometimes, disk cacheing procedures recommend reducing the number of buffers. In this case, don't simply delete the BUFFERS command, because you will get the default of 15. It's better to use a minimal figure like 2.

CD

Used to change directories (CHDIR is the full command).

Format:

```
CD path
```

CLS

This command CLears the Screen.

Format:

```
CLS
```

Comments:

The screen is reset to grey characters on a black background, unless you have previously selected others with ANSI.SYS (see PROMPT).

COPY

Use this to copy files, which can come from the screen or a disk, and go to a screen, disk drive or printer (for example, you can COPY, instead of TYPE, a file to the screen).

Format:

```
COPY [switch] source [switch] destina-
tion [option]
```

Comments:

You don't have to copy files just to disk. You can also copy them (text files only) to the screen for viewing (instead of TYPE), to a serial port for transmission or to a parallel port for printing. For instance:

```
COPY FRED CON
```

would display the file FRED on your screen (as with TYPE), while:

```
COPY FRED PRN
```

would print it.

You can change the name of a file as you copy it:

```
COPY C:FRED A:TOM
```

will copy FRED from C to A, and call it TOM.

Notes:

You can't copy a file to itself. Copying a file to a destination where one with the same name already exists will overwrite the existing file, with no prompting.

Be careful not to delete files after you've copied them until you are sure the operation has been carried out successfully. For example, copying all files in a directory (that is, *.*) into another seems simple enough until you mistype the name of the destination directory, which to the system will mean that the directory specified won't exist. In that case COPY will assume the contents are destined for one (very big) file and proceed to make it. However, if *program* files are included in the list, and you haven't included the /B option (meaning binary), they will be truncated at the first end-of-file marker.

COUNTRY

The country code (in CONFIG.SYS) tells DOS to use the date, time, currency format and code page used by your country.

Format:

```
COUNTRY=nnn,cp,[d:]\path\COUNTRY.SYS
```

Comments:

nnn is one of the following codes (loosely based on the telephone system):

061	Australia	032	Belgium
002	Canada (Fr)	045	Denmark
358	Finland	033	France
049	W Germany	035	Hungary
972	Israel	039	Italy
081	Japan	082	Korea
003	Latin America	785	Middle East
031	Netherlands	047	Norway
351	Portugal	007	Russia
034	Spain	046	Sweden
041	Switzerland	090	Turkey
044	United Kingdom	001	United States

cp is the code page, if different from the one associated with the code above.

Notes:

Country codes do not concern themselves with keyboards; use **KEYB.**

DEL

A built-in command, used to delete files.

Format:

```
DEL [filespec] [options]
```

Comments:

If you try to delete all files in a directory, as when using wildcard characters (*.*), you will see a message like:

```
Are you sure (Y/N)?
```

Type *Y* to go ahead; *N* if you change your mind.

This command does not query you before erasing a file, so the file deleted is not recoverable except under certain special circumstances (see Notes, below).

Notes:

A deleted file isn't actually erased from the disk; instead, the directory list is modified to show that the space occupied by the file is available for use. Provided that space has not been used again, it is sometimes possible (using a suitable recovery program) to recover a file once you've deleted it.

DIR

DIR displays the contents of a disk directory.

Format:

```
DIR [d:][filespec]
```

Comments:

Typing DIR by itself will show all files (that is, *.*) allowed to be shown in the *current* directory, together with the names of any subdirectories. Wildcards (* or ?) can filter the files selected. For instance, you can show only .TXT files by filtering them with the command:

```
DIR *.TXT
```

DISKCOPY

This command copies entire diskettes of the same format, producing complete clones, sector by sector.

Format:

```
DISKCOPY [source] [destination] [options]
```

Comments:

If you only have one drive, DISKCOPY prompts you to swap disks at the right time.

Example:

```
DISKCOPY A: B:
```

copies the contents of disk A: to drive B.

Notes:

You cannot use DISKCOPY with a fixed disk, a floating drive or a remote drive. Certain diskette types cannot be copied properly in certain drive types. The following are supported (but see also the System Manual):

```
5.25"

DS DD 40T 360Kb
DS DD 80T 1.2Mb

3.5"

DS DD 80T 720Kb
DS DD 80T 1.44 Mb
```

where DS = Double sided, DD = Double Density, so:

- a 360Kb drive can only copy 360K diskettes

- a 1.2Mb drive can copy 1.2Mb and 360K diskettes

- a 720Kb drive can only copy 720K diskettes

- a 1.44Mb drive can copy 720K and 1.44Mb diskettes

Although a 1.2Mb drive can copy 360Kb diskettes, you may not be able to read them in a 360Kb drive, because the track width is half the size in the higher capacity drive, and the (wider) lower capacity drive heads will read both the old information and the new that is written down the middle of the (old) track.

If you want to copy between dissimilar diskette types, use XCOPY, which will copy subdirectories, but don't forget to make the volume labels match (use the /L switch).

ECHO

Controls the display of text on screen, typically used in batch files for including messages and prompts as part of the startup procedure.

Format:
```
ECHO ON|OFF
ECHO [=] [message]
```

Comments:

ECHO can display any printable ASCII character and is ON by default. The line ECHO OFF in a batch file stops all subsequent lines of it being shown on screen as they are executed (individual lines in a batch file can be suppressed by placing @ as the first character).

Some program messages, such as:

```
1 File(s) copied
```

and errors, are displayed regardless of the current ECHO status. Suppress these by adding >NUL at the end of the relevant line (NUL is the computer equivalent of a black hole to which such messages are despatched).

FORMAT

This command initialises diskettes.

Format:

```
FORMAT [d:][options]
```

Comments:

The diskette contents will be completely erased.

Formatting takes place to the highest capacity of the drive used, which can be varied by using options as described below.

Options:

/4   Forces 360k format (on 1.2 Mb drives).

/F   Sets the capacity of the drive to be formatted, using the form: /F:*size* (/F:720 will format 720k diskettes in a 1.44 Mb drive).

/S   Copies system files onto the formatted diskette.

Drives supported:

Only the most common types are described:

```
5.25"

DS DD 40T 360Kb
DS DD 80T 1.2Mb

3.5"

DS DD 80T 720Kb
DS DD 80T 1.44 Mb
```

where DS = Double Sided, DD = Double Density.

Example:

To format a 720k (Double Density) diskette in a 1.44 Mb (High Density) 3.5 inch drive, type:

```
FORMAT A: /F:720
```

Notes:

FORMAT will not work with networked drives, or assignments created with ASSIGN or SUBST.

KEYB

A device driver that loads national keyboard settings.

Format:

    KEYB xx

Comments:

xx is a two-letter country code. The versions supported are given below, together with their two-character codes (and code page):

Belgium	BE	(437)	Canada (Fr)	CF	(863)
Denmark	DK	(865)	Finland	SU	(437)
France	FR	(437)	Germany	GR	(437)
Hungary	HU	(852)	Italy	IT	(437)
Lat America	LA	(437)	Netherlands	NL	(437)
Norway	NO	(865)	Portugal	PO	(860)
Russia	RU	(866)	Spain	SP	(437)
Sweden	SV	(437)	Swiss (Fr)	SF	(437)
Swiss (Ge)	SG	(437)	Turkey TF	TQ	(857)
UK	UK	(437)	USA	US	(437)

MD

Use MD to create directories.

Format:

    MD[\][d:]dirpath

Example:

If you want to create subdirectory \WP from the root directory, enter:

    MD\WP

Notes:

It's very easy to create a directory to copy files into and then forget to change to it, thus getting the new files right where you don't want them (usually the Root directory) – don't forget to *change to the new directory* (with CD) *after creating it!*

PATH

Allows you to set up a standard search routine for programs or batch files (not data or overlay files — see APPEND) which cannot be found in the current directory. The named directories will be searched in the order you enter them with this command. If the programs are still not locatable, you must specify the full *filespec* to run them.

Format:

```
PATH [[d:]dirpath [;[d:]dirpath]... |;]
```

Comments:

A semicolon is used to separate directories on one command line (see example).

Example:

To set a multiple path command in AUTOEXEC.BAT, use the form:

```
PATH C:\OSUTILS;\DRDOS;\WS;\WP
```

Notes:

This command is used for .COM, .EXE or .BAT files, and is usually run from AUTOEXEC.BAT.

For best performance, use the least number of paths, so that the system doesn't have to search through multiple layers of subdirectories.

Use a batch file for each program which resets the path as required (some programs need the DOS path to find their own files). You can then collect all the batch files into one directory and only have that in the path specified in AUTOEXEC.BAT.

If you do end up with a long path, and you need more, you can always continue with APPEND, or use SUBST to swap a drive letter for a path description.

See also SET.

PROMPT

PROMPT modifies the command prompt with special commands beginning with $.

Format:

```
PROMPT [promptstring]
```

Comments:

The prompt can also carry out a command every time it displays.

Typing PROMPT by itself resets the default (ng). The *promptstring* can contain valid ASCII characters, or these symbols preceded by $:

d	The date.
g	The > character.
p	The current directory.
t	The time.
—	Carriage Return and Line Feed; i.e. go to beginning of a new line. You can also use a hyphen (-).

Examples:

Navigation around directories is made considerably easier by modifying the prompt to show you the current directory.

```
PROMPT $p$g
```

will display (for example):

```
c:\DOS>
```

This is the most common variation of the screen prompt, but you can also include the date, time and many other commands, e.g.:

```
PROMPT $t$d
```

Try this one for size (all on one line, and you will need ANSI.SYS loaded):

```
PROMPT $e[1;64H$e[1;33;44m$d
$e[1;1H$e[1;33;44m$t $h$h$h$h$h$h Time
$e[0m$e[25;1H$e[1;33;44m$p$g$e[0m
```

RD

RD removes directories, provided they are empty.

Format:

```
RD [d:]dirpath
```

Comments:

To remove a directory, the following conditions must be satisfied:

- It must be empty (check for hidden files).

- It cannot be a current directory on any drive (that is, you cannot be inside the directory you wish to delete).

- It cannot be assigned to floating drives; that is, no SUBST or JOIN command can be in force.

Examples:

To erase directory SUB3:

```
RD SUB1\SUB2\SUB3
```

REM

REM is used to add comments (that are not displayed) to batch files, including CONFIG.SYS, so you can understand the horrible mess much later on when you've forgotten what you wrote in the first place.

Format:

```
REM [comment]
```

Comments:

The maximum length of a *comment* is 123 characters (plus REM) — you can actually type more if you want, but only 123 will be shown on the screen.

The semi-colon is an alias for REM.

REN

Changes the name of a file.

Format:
```
REN oldfile.ext newfile.ext
```

Comments:

The wildcard characters (* and ?) can be used, for example, to rename all files having a .IN extension as files with .OUT extensions.:

```
REN *.IN *.OUT
```

You can't rename a file to an existing name.

To set a variable, just use it as supplied (e.g. SET VER = 3.31). For testing purposes, it needs to be surrounded by "% on either side, e.g. "%..%", as in:

SHELL

An environment variable that tells applications where COMMAND.COM is.

Format:
```
SHELL = filespec [options]
```

Options:

/E:nnnnn	The size of the environment in bytes, where *nnnnn* is in the range 256-32751. Most times, the environment size can safely be reduced to, say, 192, which will gain a few extra bytes of memory for applications. Every little helps!
/P	Fixes this copy of this command processor permanently in memory (usually the first one loaded). In addition, the AUTO-EXEC.BAT file is automatically run.
/F	Automatically answers "F" to the error message "Abort, Retry, Fail?"

TYPE

TYPE displays the contents of a *text* file on your screen. You can use the wildcard characters (* and ?) to type multiple files. The effect is the same as copying a file to the screen.

Format:

```
TYPE filespec [options]
```

Comments:

Press < Ctrl > -S to stop the display from scrolling, and again to restart. < Ctrl > -C aborts the display.

Another way of sending file contents to the printer is:

```
TYPE filename.ext PRN
```

XCOPY

An extended version of COPY; it selectively copies files and whole subdirectories.

Format:
```
XCOPY [@]filespec [dirpath] [options]
```

Comments:

The *filespec* is the drive, path and name of the files to be copied (wildcard characters are allowed). The *dirpath* is the destination drive and path to which the files will be copied. XCOPY is intelligent enough to create a new directory on the destination if you have specified one that doesn't exist.

Whereas COPY deals only with individual parts of a file at a time and is therefore continually waiting for floppy disk drives to get up to speed, XCOPY will read in as many files as memory allows, and write them to the destination in one continuous stream. This makes it extremely useful in backup procedures, as it retains files in a useable condition.

Options:

/E   Create subdirectories, even if they are empty (see also /S).

/H   Include system files. The default is to ignore them.

/L   Copies the disk label as well as the files (great for diskcopying with different sizes).

/S   Copy files from subdirectories and maintain structure (use with /E if you want all subdirectories).

/V   Verify that data is written correctly.

Example:

To copy all files with a .LET extension from the C:\WP directory, which has two subdirectories, \WP\FRED and \WP\MARY, to a diskette in drive A, and when you want to preserve the same subdirectory structure, use the command:

```
XCOPY \wp\*.let A: /S /E
```

DOS files you don't normally need (and what they do).

.CPI files

Code Page Information files, used to vary screen and printer output for the country you're in. Get rid of them by typing **DEL *.CPI**.

.BAS files

Used for BASIC, and boring. **DEL *.BAS**.

ANSI.SYS

Used to change how the screen looks and what the keyboard does. If your programs don't need it to display screens correctly (check the manual), delete it.

APPEND

Tells the system what directories (other than the current one) it should look in for data files (e.g. those not covered by the PATH command, which is only used for .COM, .EXE or .BAT files), so you can open data files as if they were in the current directory rather than elsewhere. However, when the file is saved, it's not put in its original place but in the *current* directory, so APPEND only helps you to *find* files in the first place. Very confusing! It's not really necessary unless your programs have problems finding their overlay files, or you want a larger PATH command.

ATTRIB

Allows manual changing of file attributes. Only useful if other people are using your machine and you want to protect your files, or you want to manually change the Archive attribute.

BACKUP

This command makes backup copies of file(s), mainly between hard and floppy disks. Unfortunately, it does so in a special format, so you can't directly use the files that have been backed up, or restore single ones (you have to restore the whole lot). BACKUP is sensitive to DOS versions, and if a disk becomes unreadable, you can't complete the RESTORE operation. Third party programs are better, and so is XCOPY.

CHKDSK	This checks a disk for space allocation and spacing errors. It does not check the surface of a disk, but only whether it presents the device structure that DOS expects.
	It can also be used for file repair, using the /F switch, but you should use this program without /F first, to ensure that you really want to fix what it finds. This is because CHKDSK is to fixing things what a pile of bricks is to the Arts, however good it might be at diagnostics. There are better solutions!
COMP	Compares files.
DEBUG	Used for debugging programs — for programmers only!
DISKCOMP	Compares two diskettes of the same format track by track.
DISPLAY.SYS	Enables code page switching for EGA and VGA displays. Mostly useless unless you really want to change the way that text looks on screen.
DOSSHELL	A pretty front end to DOS that does many tasks on your behalf. Has many associated files as well. Sort of useful, but not a replacement for Windows.
DRIVER.SYS	Used in CONFIG.SYS, allows DOS to work with strange disk drives.
DRIVPARM	Allows you to specify the characteristics of a disk drive so that DOS can use it.
EDLIN	A primitive text editor supplied with every version of (MS) DOS; use only in dire necessity!
EXE2BIN	Converts .EXE (executable) programs into .BIN (binary image) or .COM (executable) files — for programmers only.
FC	Compares files.

FDISK	Used to split hard disks into partitions (*not* directories). The DR DOS version formats the hard disk as well. For technical people only!
FIND	FIND looks for text strings in text files and displays the lines containing them. Useful if you're continually forgetting what's on your hard disk.
GRAFTABL	Displays extended graphics characters and code pages on CGA monitors. But you've got VGA anyway, haven't you?
GRAPHICS	This is used to print a graphics display on to an IBM-compatible graphics printer, using the < **PrtScr** > key.
GWBASIC	A BASIC program used to create and run .BAS files. Useful for programming, but little else.
JOIN	Makes a complete drive structure appear to be a subdirectory of another drive (related to SUBST, which allocates a drive letter to a directory path).
MSHERC	Does things to Hercules monitors.
NLSFUNC	Provides support for extended country information so you can use CHCP to change code pages.
PACKING.LST	A list of files supplied with DOS.
PRINTER.SYS	Switches code pages for IBM printers.
QBASIC	A BASIC program used to create and run .BAS files. Useful for programming, but little else; however, it is required by DOS 5 to run the EDIT text editing program.
RECOVER	Dangerous, this!
	It's supposed to recover files from a damaged disk, and if used with a *particular* filename can be successful.

However...... under other circumstances, all your subdirectory entries will be rewritten as files, and you won't be able to get to the files that were in your subdirectories!

DON'T use wildcards with RECOVER — every file will be renamed and you won't be able to remember what they used to be!

Delete this and use a third party program instead (even on floppies).

REPLACE | REPLACE copies selected files from one place to another; it's like COPY, but sensitive to target files. For example, you can update previous versions of files, so it may be useful for updating software, but little else.

RESTORE | Restores directories and files that have been backed up with BACKUP. If you don't use BACKUP, you don't need this.

SETVER | Allows DOS to report a different version number when interrogated by programs. Sometimes needed.

SHARE | This provides support for file locking, so files can be shared between programs, or you can load more than one copy of a program. With some versions of DOS (i.e. 4), it's needed to cope with large hard disks.

SID | The DR DOS version of DEBUG.

SORT | A filter program that reads data, sorts it alphabetically and writes it again.

TOUCH | TOUCH changes the time and date stamps of files.

TREE | TREE gives a picture of your directory structure.

VIEWMAX | The DR DOS equivalent of DOSSHELL. Has many associated files.

Appendix B

Glossary

Access time In relation to hard disks and memory, the average time taken to deliver information starting from the original request for it. The lower this number is, the more efficient the system.

Analogue signal An electrical signal that varies according to the characteristics of the information it represents. Volume is a good example, where a louder sound is represented by a higher voltage, or is *analogous* to it, hence the name.

Analogue transmission is used on the telephone line and is not compatible with computer signals, which are digital.

ANSI American National Standards Institute; a body that lays down standards for computer products.

Apple A company famous for the Macintosh range of computers, which are *not* IBM-compatible, although they have some ability to read IBM disks.

Application Program Any program used to do work on your computer, such as a wordprocessor.

ASCII Acronym for *American Standard Code for Information Interchange* (pronounced "ask-ee"). Almost all the alphabetical characters used in the world have been given numbers as part of a standard code, so that printers can do the same job wherever they are. The software concerned sends an ASCII code to the printer, which prints characters according to the numbers it receives.

Instant ASCII files are created by sending the characters to disk instead of the printer, hence the "printing to disk" option in most programs. Note that the format of a file treated this way is not the same as the original file, even though the text contents might be.

A side benefit of this standardisation is that you can exchange data between programs that understand ASCII, where they wouldn't normally be able to. ASCII is used as a bridge, in this case.

There are 128 ASCII characters, of which 32 are reserved as control characters.

ASCII File   One which contains only ASCII-coded characters, typically obtained when you print a file to disk, although most programs can export data directly in ASCII.

AT   The designation given to the successor to the IBM PC (stands for Advanced Technology). Originally 286-based, but also covers 386-based PCs as well.

AT Bus   The 16-bit expansion bus found on AT computers and above.

AT Command Set   An industry standard group of modem commands, each of which must be preceded by the letters AT in order to get the modem's attention (as used by Hayes). For instance ATDP tells the modem to dial (D) with pulses (P) the number that follows.

Attributes   Electronic flags associated with a file that indicate its status to the system, such as whether it's Hidden, Read-Only, System, etc.

AUTOEXEC .BAT   A system configuration batch file that is run after COMMAND.COM is loaded, containing commands that *run under DOS* to set up your computer. See also CONFIG.SYS, which performs a similar function, but is run before the second hidden system file is run.

Background operations   In multi-tasking, such as with Windows, the lowest priority work the computer will perform at the same time as anything else. Some programs can communicate in the background; i.e. get on with passing data to another computer while you're using your wordprocessor.

Backing up   The process of making a security copy of a file or files on to separate media (e.g. from a hard disk to a floppy or tape).

Backup   A duplicate copy of a program or data, so you have a spare.

Base memory   The 640K of memory traditionally allocated for programs, data and the operating system to run inside.

Batch file   An ASCII text file containing a sequence of commands, batched together for convenience, to save you typing the commands one after the other.

Each line is interpreted as a command, unless the letters REM (for REMark) are at the beginning.

A batch file must have a .BAT extension.

Baud rate A measurement of the rate of signal changes per second. It is normally equal to bits-per-second, so the two terms can be used in place of each other as one bit is generally transmitted per signal change. However, with fast modems, the number of bits transmitted per second will not coincide with signal changes because of *data compression*; a 2400 *bits per second* transmission rate may actually be transmitting at 600 *baud*.

Both transmitter and sender need to have the same Baud rate to communicate successfully.

Benchmark A test of performance by which other software or hardware is measured.

Binary The native language of all computers. Numbers, letters, and instructions are represented in 1s and 0s (or ONs and OFFs) inside the computer.

Binary File Another name for a file containing program code, as opposed to an ASCII file.

BIOS A computer's Basic Input/Output System is programming code written in ROM which is used by DOS or programs to reach specific parts of the hardware. It is specially written for the hardware it is in and permanently installed. Its function is to make the computer look to DOS like a standard IBM.

ROMs are slow, however, and it is possible to copy the code into RAM so that execution is faster. You could use fast ROMs, but these are expensive. See Shadow RAM.

Bit Contraction for **BI**nary digi**T**. A single 1 or 0 switch and the smallest unit of unambiguous information used in a digital computer. Patterns of bits represent characters or symbols. Eight bits make a byte, and it takes one byte of data to create a character on screen.

Boot Short for "bootstrapping", which means starting the computer up, usually at the beginning of the day's work.

Buffer A small amount of memory which temporarily holds data until it can be transmitted or processed by another device, thus compensating for the different speeds of various parts of a computer. On an IBM PC, a buffer is 512 bytes in size, which equals a sector on a disk.

Bug A hardware or software error. The word was first coined from early computer days when a singed butterfly was found to have clogged up the works of a computer.

Built-in command A command integral to the operating system, meaning that you won't find a corresponding filename on disk.

Bulletin Board An electronic mail service that acts like a noticeboard, typically provided by computer enthusiasts or other special interest groups, but increasingly used by companies and the like to provide sales or technical support.

A bulletin board is simply a computer that allows people to call it up over the telephone and to pass information back and forth. The machine itself has to be left on all the time, or at least for the time the board is supposed to be open, and have an auto-answer modem installed.

Burn-in The process of a screen image being permanently imprinted into the phosphor inside the tube, which appears as a "ghost" image behind the displays of other programs. This typically happens when you leave a program continually displaying the same screen.

Bus A path for electrical signals, as in data bus, which is actually a collection of separate electrical paths working together, since data inside the computer is transmitted in parallel. Along the bus are sent timing, data and address signals so that devices situated on the bus can communicate with each other in the proper fashion.

Byte The basic measurement unit of computer memory, or a collection of bits. A byte consists of eight ON or OFF switches or bits which are handled as one unit. Each character or number is represented by one byte.

Cache Cacheing bridges the speed gap between various parts of the computer. A small amount of memory, similar in concept to a buffer, that sits between disk drives (or memory) and the CPU to hold data in anticipation that it will be used again.

Accessing data tends to be sequential, so it's a fair bet that what you want next is next in line. The cache's job is to make intelligent guesses as to what data you want next and load it into cache memory, so that next time your data comes from the fast cache and not from the slower parts. The cache must be intelligent, otherwise it performs merely the same function as a buffer.

Central Processing Unit (CPU)	The main unit of a computer which interprets and executes instructions that are fed to it from memory.
Chooser	The program used on a Macintosh to choose between printers and other services available on that machine, especially on a network.
Clock Speed	A measure of how fast a computer runs. It is the speed at which instructions are carried out on a PC, regulated by a crystal that vibrates at a particular frequency. The speed is expressed in terms of MegaHertz, or MHz, but think of it of miles per hour.
Code Page	The collection of letters, numbers and symbols specific to a language collected into one table. If you need to change languages to use your keyboard or printer properly, just switch code pages.
Com1/Com2	The names of the first and second serial ports on an IBM-compatible.
Command	What you tell the computer to do, usually embodied in a small program.
Command Line	Where you issue your commands on the screen, next to the prompt, although the term could also mean the complete command, plus any variations in the form of switches.
Command switch	A means of varying a command issued to the computer, intended to change the way it operates, typically used in conjunction with a forward stroke (/). For example, issuing the command DIR with a /P switch displays the directory a pageful at a time.
COM Port	Short for communications port, through which a computer can talk to the outside world, including other computers.
CONFIG .SYS	A configuration file, inspected by DOS before it looks at AUTO-EXEC.BAT, that gives DOS information about the kinds of hardware attached to your computer. The commands in it actually become *part of DOS*, rather than run under DOS.
Control character	A character of the alphabet used for functional purposes rather than signifying text. For example, < Ctrl-S > may be used to temporarily halt scrolling of a screen display.
Conventional Memory	Also known as *Base Memory*, memory addressable by an Intel CPU in *Real Mode*, totalling 640K. DOS operates in Real Mode, so having more than this is useless unless you have a memory manager capable of switching the chip into and out of protected mode so you can use more than this.

CP/M Control Program for Microcomputers; the predecessor to DOS, used on machines based around the Z80 microchip.

Current drive See *Logged Drive*.

Cut and Paste The process of deleting parts of a document and inserting them elsewhere, either into the same document or another.

Daisywheel The part of a printer that contains moulded characters and which strikes the ribbon to mark the paper. Daisywheels can be changed to supply different typefaces.

Data Information expressed in a formalised way (usually digital) for processing by computers.

Data compression A way of making data fit into a smaller space when transmitting, so you save connection charges.

Default A value assumed by the system until changed (as in default drive).

Device Hardware (e.g. a printer or modem) attached to a computer.

Device driver Sometimes devices cannot be operated directly by the system, possibly because they operate in a non-standard way. A device driver is software that is loaded alongside the system to make sure the device is run properly — the software then becomes part of DOS. Device drivers are usually identifiable by their .SYS extension.

Directory Part of a disk in which files are stored, or the list of files on a disk (see the DIR command).

Disk Cache See *Cache*.

Disk mirroring This is a procedure that writes your data to a secondary hard disk at the same (or as close as possible to) the time it is written to your primary disk. Thus, if one fails, your work can immediately be found on the other (which becomes a Godsend if your system fails only five minutes before the scheduled backup time!).

The sort of intelligent disk controller used for this will perform cacheing as well, so a typical impact on performance is likely to be less than about 5% if two disks have to be handled at once.

DMA *Direct Memory Access* is a system which allows disk drives or other devices to pass information directly to memory without involving the Central Processor, which speeds the system up considerably. There will be at least one chip given the job of DMA Controller to oversee the process.

DOS	Disk Operating System
DOS Extender	A layer of software between DOS and an application program which allows the application to operate outside Real Mode and thus gain access to extended memory. DOS Extenders only work on 80286 and above processors.
Dot matrix	A system of printing where combinations of needles impact against a ribbon to produce characters on paper.
EISA	*Extended Industry Standard Architecture*. The normal 16-bit bus is known as the ISA bus, or Industry Standard Architecture. Its capabilities are limited when it comes to working with 32-bit chips, so the EISA bus, which is 32-bit, was designed to cope with it.
Electronic Mail	The nearest we have yet to the paperless office – you could think of it as space-age telex. Technically, the term embraces all activities relating to the sending of data of any sort through computer terminals and any equipment that may be attached to them, but these days it's generally accepted as meaning the use of a service that provides a little more, such as providing a "mailbox" where messages can be "posted" to you – in other words, a small space inside a host computer that is set aside for your use in the same way that a normal mailbox is used.
Em dash	Used in typesetting (and hence Desk Top publishing), an Em dash is the same width as the point size of the text. Em dashes are used with clauses.
En dash	Used in typesetting (and hence Desk Top publishing), an En dash is the width of the letter n. Numbers use En dashes between them.
Environment	A small area of memory (usually 1K) set aside to contain information about the status of the different parts of the computer.
	Applications can then use this information to govern the way they behave. For example, some programs can interrogate the environment to find out which version of the operating system is running (VER) or where to look to find any files requested by the operator (PATH).
EPS	*Encapsulated Postscript*, which is a format used to exchange images between graphic programs. An EPS file should (in theory) be able to be printed by copying it directly to a Postscript printer.
Error correction	A way of making sure that mistakes aren't made when transmitting data.

ESDI   *Enhanced Small Device Interface.* A connection method for larger hard disks that delivers a data throughput of 10 Mbps or more. A faster derivative of the ST-506 disk interface.

Expanded Memory   An old (hardware based) way of using more than 640K of memory on IBM-compatibles that can only address 1 Mb, which basically means 8086-based. It works by switching 16K chunks of data through a 64K area of Upper Memory called a *page frame.* The page frame ends up behaving like a window between the two areas.

Some programs still expect to use expanded memory, so modern memory managers emulate the bank-switching by converting extended memory with a device driver, usually called EMM386.something.

Expansion Slot   A space on the data bus in which you can plug an expansion board.

Extended Memory   On an Intel-based system, that above 1 Mb, addressable only in protected mode.

External Command   Commands not frequently used, and thus not automatically loaded as part of the operating system. Instead, they are stored in the DOS directory and called up as and when required.

FAT   See *File Allocation Table.*

File   A separately identifiable collection of data, either ASCII or binary; that is, text or program code. A file's details are displayed on screen when the DIR command is issued.

File Allocation Table   Commonly called the FAT, this is where the system looks first to find the location of any files on the disk to which it relates. People outside the computer industry would call it an index of any files on a disk.

Filespec   The filename and extension of a file, separated by a full stop.

Fixed disk   See *Hard Disk.*

Floppy disk   A flexible storage medium which is removable and portable for safety reasons. There are two physical sizes (5.25" and 3.5"), but how much data you can get on them really depends on how the computer they are used in makes use of them. This is why formatting is required before they are used, so they match the computer's capabilities.

Folder   The Macintosh equivalent of a directory.

Font   Technically, a variation of a typeface, but frequently used to mean the typeface itself.

Footer   Text repeated at the bottom of every page of a document. Usually it will have at least the page number and possibly the title of the document.

Format   To prepare a disk for use by a computer. A low-level format marks out the tracks and sectors and a high-level format renders the disk useable by the operating system, so this is where boot sectors, file allocation tables and the like are created. On a floppy, both operations are carried out at the same time.

Formatting is sometimes called *initialisation*.

GEM   An early attempt by Digital Research to produce a Graphical User Interface.

Hard Card   A plug-in card used in a computer that contains a complete hard disk and supporting circuitry.

Hard Disk   A permanently rotating disk, or series of disks, in a metal case filled with inert gas. It is faster and bigger than a floppy disk, and demands some discipline to manage properly, but the benefits well outweigh the disadvantages.

Hard disk performance is usually measured in terms of raw speed, but data throughput is actually dependent on other parts of the system it is installed in, and can be the real bottleneck at times.

Hayes commands   Electronic instructions to modems, used to save you pushing buttons. They were developed by Hayes in the USA but have now become a standard.

Hayes commands can be used to set your equipment to the proper speeds and even dial the number for you. When a communications program loads, it sends an *initialisation string* containing the commands needed to wake the modem up.

Hayes compatibility   The ability of a modem to conform to the standards laid down by Hayes, ranging from just recognising the commands to full emulation.

Headers   The same as footers, but at the top of the page.

Hertz   Cycles per second.

Hexa-decimal	This is a system that counts to the base sixteen, which suits computers very well, as they operate in units of eight bits at a time. However, humans count in units of ten, which causes confusion when the two are mixed and you want to express numbers greater than ten. To get around this problem, the letters A, B, C, D, E and F are substituted for 10, 11, 12, 13, 14 and 15 respectively.
High Memory (HMA)	The High Memory Area is the first 64K of extended memory (less 16 bytes for technical reasons) which is able to be accessed in Real Mode, thus providing a little more memory than the traditional 640K.
Hotkey	A key, or combination of keys, used to initiate a process, typically activating a memory-resident program.
Hz	Short for *Hertz*.
Initialisation string	A series of command characters sent to a Hayes-compatible modem to set it up ready for use, typically sent by a communications software as it loads.
Input	Information entered into a computer, such as what you type at the keyboard.
Insert mode	A state of the computer's operation whereby text appearing on screen pushes aside any already there.
Instruction set	Commands recognised by a particular microprocessor.
Internal command	A frequently used command that is loaded with the operating system. See *Built-in command*.
I/O	Abbreviation for Input/Output.
ISA	Industry Standard Architecture, or the name given to the design of the 16-bit bus in the AT and its compatibles.
ISDN	Integrated Services Digital Network. A method of allowing the (analogue) telephone system to carry digitally encoded integrated signals containing voice data and video information, eliminating the need for modems.
	The idea is to be able to transmit simultaneous voice and data transmissions, so you can see and speak to someone at the same time.
	The data travels 25% faster, so your phone bills are cheaper (in theory).

K or KB   Abbreviation for Kilobyte (1,024 bytes).

Kilobyte   1,024 bytes or characters (actually 2 to the 10th power).

Label   Either the name given to a disk (*Volume Label*) or a marker within a batch file.

LAN   Short for *Local Area Network*.

LIM Memory   Expanded Memory conforming to the standards laid down by Lotus, Intel and Microsoft.

List device A device used to list data, typically a printer.

Local Area Network A network which provides communication between terminals in a defined area, typically in one building or a floor in that building.

Locking   A method of protecting shared data. When a file is opened, file locking prevents simultaneous access by someone else.

Logical   A word meaning "pretend", as in *logical drive*. A better word is *notional*.

Logged drive The drive at which the operating system is currently looking, or the one which it is currently logged on to (sometimes known as the *default drive*).

Lower memory The bottom part of Base Memory where the operating system is traditionally loaded. However, this takes up space that could be used for programs, so later versions of DOS have the ability to load into High Memory instead, thus keeping out of the way.

M or MB   One million bytes (1,048,576). Abbreviation for *MegaByte*.

Macro   The process of allocating a series of kcystrokes to just one or two, which saves typing after the macro has been created. Macros in a database are called *procedures*; in DOS *batch processing*; in communications programs *scripts*.

Mailmerge   Producing standard letters with a wordprocessor, where the name, address and other details may change with each copy, so each letter looks as if it's been specially prepared. Another file containing the changing data is created (typically a mailing list), and the two files are merged, hence the name.

Mains spike A short term disturbance in the mains power supply, typically occurring when other equipment on the same system is switched on (it seems to happen most often with refrigerators — you can hear the spike through your Hi Fi).

Maths Coprocessors Central Processors can only deal with whole numbers; fractions and decimals are converted to integers, calculated upon and reconverted back to the original state, which is not good for performance.

A maths coprocessor is designed to handle *floating point* numbers, where the position of the decimal point can vary. In this way it takes the load off the Central Processor and makes calculating quicker. However, software must be written to take advantage of the coprocessor, or it will have no effect at all.

Megabyte One million bytes (2 to the 20th power; 1,048,576).

Memory Temporary storage for programs and data, which is lost when the computer is switched off.

Memory Resident A feature of a program that allows it, once loaded into memory, to remain there until the power is turned off or the computer is reset.

Menu A screen display that lists choices available to you and allowing selection with keystrokes.

Menu driven Where all a program's operations are carried out through a menu system.

Micro processor The correct name for the brains of a PC, although often called *Central Processors* instead. In an IBM compatible, this will be an Intel-based chip. Macintoshes use Motorolas.

Micro Channel A 32-bit design of a data bus, proprietary to IBM and incompatible with anything else. EISA is a direct competitor, which also accepts ISA expansion cards. Although actually called Micro Channel Architecture, the initials (MCA) also stand for *Music Corporation of America* so, to avoid confusion, the word *Architecture* has been dropped.

Mirroring A method of increasing fault tolerance where all activity on one hard disk is duplicated within a very short time on another. Not the same as *duplexing*, where two different sets of hardware are used.

MNP This stands for *Microcom Networking Protocol*, after the company that invented it. It's used for error correction over telephone lines, and has been through several versions. Versions 1, 2, 3 and 4 are in the Public Domain, and can actually be emulated by software.

MNP 5 also includes data compression as well as error correction, and there is some compatibility with *V42*, so either standard can be used at each end (the same protocol must be used at both ends of a communications channel).

Don't use MNP with .ZIP files, as they will actually take longer to transmit, so upload or download them with MNP off.

Mode   A method of operation or a phase of program operation.

Modem   Acronym for MOdulator-DEModulator. A device which translates computer compatible signals into those used by the telephone, and vice versa.

Modems must be approved to work over the telephone lines, otherwise they may interfere with the operation of the telephone system.

American modems use Bell tones, whereas European ones use CCITT, so the noises they make are different and will not be understood by the respective systems. Don't use an American modem in Europe unless it's capable of switching between the two.

USA RJ11 (telephone) plugs have the active lines as the centre ones, whereas British ones use the outside ones.

Motherboard   The major circuit board in a computer that contains all the other components.

Multi Tasking   The ability of a computer to do several jobs at the same time (or concurrently, if you want to be posh). This is not the same as *task-switching*, where programs in the background are merely suspended; with multi-tasking, every program is actually running, whether in the foreground or not.

Multi-user   The ability to have more than one person using a computer at the same time.

Network   A system of computers connected together so that they can share items like printers or databases.

Notional   See *Logical*.

Nubus   The name given to the architecture on which expansion slots in the Macintosh II family of computers are based; it's not designed by Apple, but Motorola, the manufacturer of the Mac's CPU.

Online	Computer-speak for being switched on and ready to process information. Usually used in relation to printers, but often used to mean that a connection is established with another computer over the telephone system.
Operating System	The software that drives your PC and which allows application programs to be run on top. If you like, it's the software that tells your machine it's a computer and not a washing machine.

It originated from all the programming routines that were needed to run the computer, but did not need to be included in every program.

DOS is used for IBM-compatibles, but others include UNIX, OS/2, VMS and System 7 for other types. |
| **OS/2** | A 32-bit operating system written by IBM that is multi-tasking. |
| **Outliner** | A program similar to a wordprocessor that allows you to place information under headings which can be moved to suit the changing of your ideas. When headings are moved, the associated text moves as well.

Headings representing your ideas can be *promoted* or *demoted* as they gain or lose importance, and they can be collapsed or otherwise to give you different overall views of the document. |
Output	As opposed to *input*, information that comes from the computer, such as on screen or a printer.
Page frame	A contiguous (that is, consecutive) 64K block of memory situated in Upper Memory used as a "window" through which data is paged between base and extended memory.
Page preview	The facility see a whole page as it would be when printed, *before* it's printed.
Parallel	A method of transmission where data is sent side by side down separate wires (in multiples of eight). Commonly used with printers.
Path	The route in the hard disk directory system that must be taken in order to find files.
Peripheral	A posh name for a *device*. Printers and modems are peripherals.
Piping	The process of making the output of one program to become the input of another.

Plotter Used for technical drawing, plotters are basically large drawing boards over which pens in a mechanical grip move, drawing on paper you place there.

Power On Self Test A set of checks that the computer goes through when it starts up to make sure everything is working correctly.

Prompt The screen display that prompts you for information or commands. The PROMPT command changes the standard prompt to your liking.

PS/2 A range of computers produced by IBM (Personal System /2).

RAM Random Access Memory, which can be read from or written to at random.

RAM Disk A portion of memory made to look and behave like a disk drive. The advantage is speed, but data is lost when the power is turned off.

Read-only A file designation that permits you to *open* a file but not *modify* it.

Read-Only Memory Memory that can only be read from, which has the advantage of being faster in operation than disks.

Read-Write A file designation that permits you to open and/or modify it.

Real-time clock A battery powered clock inside a computer that keeps track of the current date and time, even when the computer is switched off.

REN *Ring Equivalence Number*, indicating the load a particular piece of equipment places on the telephone system. Each line can handle up to the number 4, so you can have four items with a REN of 1.

RS232C A standard for serial communications, originally for use on telephone lines, but also widely used to connect printers and plotters.

Scanners These are the reverse of printers; they take a photograph of a picture or text and convert it into a form that can be used by the computer (a bit like a photocopier). To make text readable after it has been scanned, however, you will need *Optical Character Recognition* (OCR) software to make it useable by a wordprocessor.

SCSI An interface used to connect devices (like hard disks) to a PC, commonly used by the Macintosh, but also used on PC compatibles.

Sector The smallest storage unit on a disk, the density being typically 17 to 34 sectors per track.

Serial Communications	A method of sending data as a single stream of pulses (one behind each other) over a cable. Slower than parallel, so not often used with printers. Also used for modems, mice and keyboards.
Serial Port	The socket on a computer that allows serial communications to take place in and out of the computer. As the computer internally communicates in parallel, the serial port converts from one to the other both ways as well.
Shadow RAM	Some systems are able to transfer the contents of ROMs into extended memory, which can be accessed faster. The RAM thus used is given the same electronic address as the original ROM (hence "Shadow"), so DOS can find things where it expects to. The CPU is not aware of this mapping, which is handled by the computer's BIOS.
	You will find that the amount of extended memory in your machine is reduced by the amount used for shadowing, assuming you have more than 1 Mb, or the 384 K of Upper Memory is able to be relocated above 1 Mb. Otherwise, you'll probably be better off disabling shadowing and using the memory for other purposes.
SIMM	Single In-line Memory Modules. A small circuit board with memory chips soldered on that fit into specially designed sockets.
Soft font	A typeface or font that is not kept in the printer's list of available fonts, but is downloaded from the computer prior to printing.
Soft reset	Restarting a PC from the keyboard (that is, without turning the power off and on again). On an IBM compatible, this involves pressing the < Ctrl >, < Alt > and < Delete > keys together (otherwise known as the three-fingered salute). On a Macintosh it can be done from the Special menu.
Spelling Checker	A small program that works with a wordprocessor that compares your text with those in a dictionary on disk and informs you of any differences. Great for preafrooding, but the dictionary doesn't contain definitions.
Stacks	Every time the processor is interrupted (i.e. when you press a key), any information the computer is currently processing is stored temporarily in a *stack* while the interruption is dealt with. If interrupts build up, and the stack area is too small, you will get a problem (and maybe even an error message).
Style sheet	A set of standard instructions that tell a program how text, etc should be laid out and a page is set up.

System prompt	A letter and symbol displayed on a terminal or console, indicating (usually) the current drive and path.
Timeouts	Timeouts bring into operation a predetermined event if another expected event does not occur in a set period. For instance, a timeout set for 6 seconds will cause a modem to hang up if nothing is heard on the telephone for that time.
Track	A circular path on a hard disk, used for storing information. Tracks consist of one or more clusters.
Typeahead	The ability of a computer to accept keystrokes in advance of a process finishing. Usually, you can type in up to eight characters before the previous instruction ceases.
Typeface	A design of printed characters.
Typeover	The opposite to *Insert mode*, where text inserted on the screen overwrites what is already there.
Upper Memory	On an IBM-compatible, the 384K area above 640K (and below 1 Mb) which is usually reserved for the computer's private use, but some parts can be used for programs under the right circumstances.
UPS	*Uninterruptible Power Supply.* Used where power failures are a problem, they consist of batteries capable of sustaining power to a computer for a fixed time, say 15 minutes, so as to endure an orderly shutdown. If power is needed for longer than that, then maybe a standby generator would be more appropriate.
User	You.
Variable	A character in a batch file that can be substituted for a filename.
Virtual memory	The word virtual always means "pretend". In this case, pretend memory is space on the hard disk made to look like memory which is used as an overspill when real memory runs out (it's the reverse of a RAM disk, where memory is made to look like a disk drive).
Virus	A virus is a program deliberately written to cause havoc on a computer — it's a kind of electronic vandalism. There are two types of virus. One infects program code and makes them impossible to run. The other infects the system area of a disk, hard or floppy, rendering it so useless that you can't find your work again. The second is the more dangerous, because at least with the first your data will be safe (viruses don't infect data).

Files that infect programs (.EXE and .COM files, in other words) insert themselves somewhere inside them and make the file longer, which is one clue to the virus's presence. Such viruses only spread when the program is run.

Boot sector viruses, or those that infect the areas that tell the system where to find files, copy the *master boot record* to another part of the disk and replaces it with itself and an instruction to load the original code. Thus, the virus is in memory before the operating system is.

Once any virus is in memory, it spreads itself allover the place. One clue to the presence of a virus in memory is a strange amount of memory available, say about 2K less than usual.

There are several programs available that disinfect your computer, but the best way out of trouble is not to get into it in the first place.

Be careful about the floppy disks you feed into your PC, and check for viruses often.

Wait state   A state of the computer's operation where the CPU is made to wait for one or two cycles to allow slower memory chips to catch up. In other words, a delay is introduced into the computer's operations to make way for slower components.

Windows   An operating environment written by Microsoft that is essentially DOS with pictures.

WYSIWYG   *What You See Is What You Get*; the process where printed output matches as near as possible the screen display.

Wide Area Network   Networks linked over a wide area, where a third party such as a telephone company may be involved in its operation.

Workstation   On a network, a PC using the resources on the network. Otherwise, a high performance workstation with advanced graphics capabilities, often used in scientific situations.

XT   The name given to the original IBM PC when it finally got a hard disk fitted to it (stands for Extended Technology). Slow, but useable for text-based programs (not very good at handling pictures).

Appendix C

Using Text Editors

You need a text editor to create or modify batch files and the like. The three described in this Appendix are supplied with their respective DOS versions, and enough instructions are given here to allow you to open, edit and save a batch file. For full information, refer to the DOS manual.

You can also use a wordprocessor, but *make sure you save the file in ASCII format* (printing to disk will have the same effect). Some wordprocessors (e.g. Wordstar) can create ASCII files directly with a special method of operation called *non-document* mode, which means simply that the text you are editing will not be in document format – there will be no special instructions for margins, word wrap and the like, just straight ASCII text with a Carriage Return and Line Feed at the end of each line.

EDLIN

This comes with all versions of MS-DOS, and is very rudimentary. It's a line editor rather than a text editor, and is used in dire emergency (or if you want to show off!).

Format:

```
EDLIN filename.ext
```

Comments:

If the file you propose to edit does not exist, you will see:

```
New file
*
```

At this point, type:

```
I
```

followed by **< Return >**, and you will see:

```
1:*
```

Simply type the text you want on line 1, press **< Return >** to go to line 2, and so on. When you've finished, type **< Ctrl > -C** to return to the asterisk prompt. Then type:

```
E
```

to end the file creation process.

If the file you designate does exist, you will see:

```
End of input file
*
```

which means that the contents of the file you want to work with have been loaded into memory. If you want to see them, type:

```
L
```

followed by **< Return >**, then type the number of the line you want to alter, also followed by **< Return >**. Edit the line as necessary.

Quick command list

?	List the commands available.
D	Delete the current line (the one with the asterisk).
I	Insert a line; use with the number of the line *before which* you want a new one; e.g. I5 for a line between 4 and 5.
<ctrl-c>	Stop editing and return to the * prompt.
E	Save the file and exit.
Q	Quit without saving.

EDITOR

A full-screen text editor that comes with DR DOS which can handle files of any size.

Format:

```
EDITOR [/Help] [d:][path][filename[.ext]]
```

Comments:

On the command line, you can add a filename (and path, if necessary) so you can bypass the opening screen:

```
EDITOR AUTOEXEC.BAT
```

If a filename is not supplied, you will be asked for it. If the file does not exist, EDITOR will ask permission to create it.

The next thing you will see is a blank editing screen.

Keys used:

Combinations of keys are used; for instance, holding down the < Ctrl > key while pressing S will move the cursor one space left through the text, while pressing < Ctrl > -D will move it one space to the right. These key combinations are commonly written as < Ctrl > -S or < Ctrl > -D, and the same system applies to all the other commands (the full list is given below). Notice that < Ctrl > -E, X, S and D form the shape of a diamond on the keyboard and move the cursor Up, Down, Left and Right respectively.

There are short cut keys, like < Insert > or < Delete >, that do the same job as some of the < Ctrl > -*key* combinations, which are also described later.

Enter text as required. There is no word wrap facility, so < Return > is needed at the end of each line.

EDITOR starts in *Insert mode*, which means that any text typed will move any already there one space to the right. To use EDITOR in *overtype* mode, where text you type in overwrites any already there, press < Ctrl > -V, or the < Insert > key if you have one. The display at the top of the screen to show you which mode you're in.

Delete:

To delete a character *at* the cursor, press < Ctrl > -G or < Delete >. The text to the right of it will shift to the left to fill the space.

To delete the character to the *left* of the cursor, type < Ctrl > -H or use the < Backspace > key.

To delete a whole word (that is, all characters up to the next space on the right), put the cursor on the first character and type < Ctrl > -T.

To delete the line the cursor is on, press < Ctrl > -Y.

Moving Pages:

Move text up or down a page (actually 14 lines) with < Ctrl > -R and < Ctrl > -C, or the < Pg Up > and < Pg Dn > keys, respectively.

Help:

Help is available at any time by pressing < F1 > or < Ctrl > -J (quit Help by pressing < Esc >).

Leaving:

When you have finished typing, you can either:

- Save your file and start a new one (< Ctrl > -KD).

- Save your file and quit EDITOR (< Ctrl > -KX)

To abandon your file and open a new one, as you would having opened the wrong file by mistake use < Ctrl > -KQ. If you have made any changes, you will be asked if you really want to abandon the file.

To leave EDITOR from the title screen, press the < Esc > key.

EDIT

The *MS-DOS Editor* (to give it its full title) comes with MS-DOS 5 and upwards, and depends on the presence of QBASIC.EXE in the same directory to operate. It can only handle files up to a certain size, but it will be OK for batch files.

Format:

```
EDIT filename.ext
```

Comments:

As soon as the edit screen is loaded, you can start typing. Normal editing keys apply; that is, you can move around the screen with the arrow keys, and < Insert >, < Delete >, < Backspace >, etc all work as they should.

Use < Shift > and the arrow keys to highlight text as a block, and < Shift > - < Delete > to cut the highlighted text. < Shift > plus < Insert > will place that text into a new location.

Help is available with **F1**.

Menus

There is a menu system that makes issuing commands easier.

All menus are accessed by pressing the < Alt > key, then the first letter of the one you need, such as **F** if you want to *Open* and *Save* files, and leave the program. Then press the highlighted letter of the command you want (mostly **O, S** or **X**).

Index

Words for the wise - from
Sigma Press

Sigma publish what is probably the widest range of computer books from any independent UK publisher. And that's not just for the PC, but for many other popular micros – Atari, Amiga and Archimedes – and for software packages that are widely-used in the UK and Europe, including Timeworks, Deskpress, Sage, Money Manager and many more. We also publish a whole range of professional-level books for topics as far apart as IBM mainframes, UNIX, computer translation, manufacturing technology and networking.

A complete catalogue is available, but here are some of the highlights:

Amstrad PCW
The Complete Guide to LocoScript and Amstrad PCW Computers – Hughes – £12.95
LocoScripting People – Clayton and Clayton – £12.95
The PCW LOGO Manual – Robert Grant – £12.95
Picture Processing on the Amstrad PCW – Gilmore – £12.95
See also Programming section for *Mini Office*

Archimedes
A Beginner's Guide to WIMP Programming – Fox – £12.95
See also: *Desktop Publishing on the Archimedes* and *Archimedes Game Maker's Manual*

Artificial Intelligence
Build Your Own Expert System – Naylor – £11.95
Computational Linguistics – McEnery – £14.95
Introducing Neural Networks – Carling – £14.95

Beginners' Guides
Computing under Protest! - Croucher – **£12.95**
Alone with a PC – Bradley – £12.95
The New User's Mac Book – Wilson – £12.95
PC Computing for Absolute Beginners – Edwards – £12.95

DTP and Graphics
Designworks Companion – Whale – £14.95
Ventura to Quark XPress for the PC – Wilmore – £19.95
Timeworks Publisher Companion – Morrissey – £12.95
Timeworks for Windows Companion – Sinclair – £14.95
PagePlus Publisher Companion – Sinclair – £12.95
Express Publisher DTP Companion – Sinclair – £14.95
Amiga Real-Time 3D Graphics – Tyler – £14.95
Atari Real-Time 3D Graphics – Tyler – £12.95

European and US Software Packages
Mastering Money Manager PC – Sinclair – £12.95
Using Sage Sterling in Business – Woodford – £12.95
Mastering Masterfile PC – Sinclair – £12.95
All-in-One Business Computing (Mini Office Professional) – Hughes – £12.95

Game Making and Playing
PC Games Bible – Matthews and Rigby – £12.95
Archimedes Game Maker's Manual – Blunt – £14.95
Atari Game Maker's Manual – Hill – £14.95
Amiga Game Maker's Manual – Hill – £16.95
Adventure Gamer's Manual – Redrup – £12.95

General

Music and New Technology – Georghiades and Jacobs – £12.95
Getting the Best from your Amstrad Notepad – Wilson – £12.95
Computers and Chaos (Atari and Amiga editions) – Bessant – £12.95
Computers in Genealogy – Isaac – £12.95
Multimedia, CD-ROM and Compact Disc – Botto – £14.95
Advanced Manufacturing Technology – Zairi – £14.95

Networks

$25 Network User Guide – Sinclair – £12.95
Integrated Digital Networks – Lawton – £24.95
Novell Netware Companion – Croucher – £16.95

PC Operating Systems and Architecture

Working with Windows 3.1 – Sinclair – £16.95
Servicing and Supporting IBM PCs and Compatibles – Moss – £16.95
The DR DOS Book – Croucher – £16.95
MS-DOS Revealed – Last – £12.95
PC Architecture and Assembly Language – Kauler – £16.95
Programmer's Technical Reference – Williams – £19.95
MS-DOS File and Program Control – Sinclair – £12.95
Mastering DesqView – Sinclair – £12.95

Programming

C Applications Library – Pugh – £16.95
Starting MS-DOS Assembler – Sinclair – £12.95
Understanding Occam and the transputer – Ellison – £12.95
Programming in ANSI Standard C – Horsington – £14.95
Programming in Microsoft Visual Basic – Penfold – £16.95
For **LOGO**, *see Amstrad PCW*

UNIX and mainframes

UNIX – The Book – Banahan and Rutter – £11.95
UNIX – The Complete Guide – Manger – £19.95
RPG on the IBM AS/400 – Tomlinson – £24.95

HOW TO ORDER

Prices correct for 1993.
Order these books from your usual bookshop, or direct from:

SIGMA PRESS,
1 SOUTH OAK LANE,
WILMSLOW, CHESHIRE, SK9 6AR

PHONE: 0625 – 531035; FAX: 0625 – 536800

PLEASE ADD £1 TOWARDS POST AND PACKING FOR ONE BOOK.
POSTAGE IS FREE FOR TWO OR MORE BOOKS.
OVERSEAS ORDERS: please pay by credit card; we will add airmail postage at actual cost

CHEQUES SHOULD BE MADE PAYABLE TO **SIGMA PRESS.**

ACCESS AND VISA WELCOME – 24 HOUR ANSWERPHONE SERVICE.